Finding Strength, Balance *and* Joy *in Your Next Chapter*

REDEFINING
Menopause

HANNA OLIVAS
Along With 21 Inspiring Authors

TABLE OF CONTENTS

INTRODUCTION

Welcome to *Redefining Menopause: Finding Strength, Balance, and Joy in Your Next Chapter*. This book is more than just a guide; it's an invitation to embrace a transformative period of your life with open arms and an open heart.

Menopause is often surrounded by misconceptions and negative narratives, but here, we aim to shift that perspective. Through heartfelt personal stories and practical strategies, we explore how this phase can be a time of renewal and empowerment. Each chapter is crafted to inspire you to not only manage the physical changes but to also cultivate emotional resilience and rediscover your passions.

You'll find holistic advice tailored to help you navigate symptoms and reclaim your sense of self. From self-care rituals to fostering connections with others who understand your journey, our goal is to provide you with the tools to flourish.

As you delve into these pages, we encourage you to reflect on your own experiences and aspirations. Together, we'll celebrate the wisdom that comes with age and the strength that resides within you. Your next chapter holds boundless potential, and we are here to support you every step of the way.

Join us as we redefine menopause—not as an ending, but as a vibrant new beginning. Your best years are just beginning, and we can't wait for you to discover the joy that awaits!

Hanna Olivas

Founder and CEO of SHE RISES STUDIOS

https://www.linkedin.com/company/she-rises-studios/
https://www.facebook.com/sherisesstudios
https://www.instagram.com/sherisesstudios_llc/
www.SheRisesStudios.com

Author, Speaker, and Founder. Hanna was born and raised in Las Vegas, Nevada, and has paved her way to becoming one of the most influential women of 2022. Hanna is the co-founder of She Rises Studios and the founder of the Brave & Beautiful Blood Cancer Foundation. Her journey started in 2017 when she was first diagnosed with Multiple Myeloma, an incurable blood cancer. Now more than ever, her focus is to empower other women to become leaders because The Future is Female. She is currently traveling and speaking publicly to women to educate them on entrepreneurship, leadership, and owning the female power within.

A Journey of Transformation, Grace, and Self-Love

By Hanna Olivas

There comes a time in every woman's life when her body begins to change in ways that may feel foreign, unfamiliar, and even a little unsettling. For many, this phase—known as menopause—has been framed as an ending, a time when youth fades, vitality wanes, and the body seems to betray the woman it has served so faithfully. But what if we redefined menopause not as an ending, but as a beginning? What if, instead of resisting it, we embraced it with grace, with love, and with the understanding that it is simply another chapter in the story of our lives?

Menopause is one of the most significant transitions a woman will go through, and how we navigate this journey can shape the rest of our lives in powerful ways. It's not a loss of womanhood or vitality; rather, it's an invitation to reconnect with ourselves, to honor our bodies, and to step into a deeper, more authentic version of who we are. This chapter will explore how to redefine menopause in a way that allows us to move through this transformation with acceptance, strength, and joy, trusting the process as a natural, beautiful part of life.

The Beginning of a New Chapter

The first step to embracing menopause is understanding that it is not the end of something, but the beginning of something new. Throughout our lives, we undergo countless transformations—puberty, pregnancy, childbirth, and the changes that come with motherhood. Each of these stages is a reminder that, as women, we are always evolving. Menopause is no different. It is not a cessation of life, but a natural transition, a rite of passage into a stage where wisdom and inner strength take center stage.

While society has often framed menopause as a time of decline, we can choose to see it through a new lens. This is a time when the demands of others may begin to quiet, allowing us to turn inward, to rediscover ourselves, and to reconnect with our desires, passions, and purpose. It is a time to step back from the busyness of life and reflect on what truly matters.

Rather than seeing menopause as something to be feared or resisted, we can approach it with curiosity and openness, recognizing that this is a unique opportunity for personal growth. This shift in perspective— seeing menopause as a beginning rather than an end—can be profoundly liberating. It gives us the freedom to embrace the changes that come with it, not with resignation, but with gratitude and anticipation for what's to come.

Embracing the Body's Wisdom

The physical symptoms of menopause—hot flashes, night sweats, fatigue, weight gain—can be challenging, but they are also a reflection of the body's incredible wisdom. Our bodies are always speaking to us, and during menopause, they speak more loudly than ever. The changes we experience are signals that it's time to slow down, to listen, and to care for ourselves in new ways.

One of the most empowering things we can do during menopause is to shift from seeing these symptoms as inconveniences to viewing them as messages. Hot flashes may be your body's way of saying, "I need you to pay attention." Fatigue may be a reminder that it's time to rest, to recharge, and to let go of the relentless pace we've often kept. By tuning into these signals, we can begin to nurture our bodies with the care and attention they deserve.

Self-care during menopause is not a luxury; it is a necessity. This is a time when the body requires more nourishment, both physically and emotionally. It's about finding what makes you feel good, what energizes you, and what brings you peace. For some, that might mean adjusting your diet to include more nutrient-rich foods that support hormonal balance. For others, it might mean finding joy in movement—whether that's yoga, walking, or dance—that helps you stay connected to your body.

Equally important is the emotional nourishment we give ourselves. Menopause can stir up many feelings—grief, frustration, confusion— but it can also bring a profound sense of peace and clarity. This is a time to offer yourself compassion, to honor your emotions without judgment, and to allow yourself the space to feel whatever comes up. In caring for yourself with this level of tenderness, you acknowledge the importance of your own well-being, and that in itself is an act of profound love.

Trusting the Process

One of the greatest lessons menopause teaches us is the importance of trusting the process. As women, we are often conditioned to control everything—to manage our schedules, our families, our careers, our health—but menopause reminds us that some things are beyond our control. The body will change, hormones will fluctuate, and some days will be more difficult than others. But in the midst of it all, there is an invitation to surrender, to let go of the need to control, and to trust that this journey is leading us somewhere beautiful.

Trusting the process doesn't mean passivity; it means releasing the idea that we have to have all the answers, that we have to "fix" menopause or make it go away. Instead, it's about accepting the changes as they come and allowing them to unfold in their own time. This is not always easy, especially when the physical symptoms are intense, but it is in this surrender that we find peace.

Learning to trust the process of menopause also means embracing the unknown. Every woman's journey through menopause is different, and there is no one-size-fits-all approach. What worked for one woman may not work for another, and that's okay. The key is to listen to your own body, to trust that it knows what it needs, and to give yourself permission to navigate this journey in the way that feels right for you.

The Emotional Journey of Menopause

Menopause is not just a physical transition; it's an emotional and spiritual one as well. As the body changes, so too do our identities. For many women, menopause is a time of reflection—a time to look back on the life they've lived so far, to honor their accomplishments, and to assess where they want to go next.

This reflection can bring up a range of emotions—joy, gratitude, sadness, and even grief. There may be a sense of mourning for the woman you once were, for the roles you once played, and for the life that is now changing. But alongside that grief can come a profound sense of liberation. As the demands of others begin to lessen, there is more space to focus on yourself, on your own dreams, and on the life you want to create moving forward.

Embracing this emotional journey is essential to moving through menopause with grace. It's about allowing yourself to feel the full spectrum of emotions without shame or judgment. It's about acknowledging that it's okay to grieve, it's okay to be frustrated, and it's okay to not have all the answers. But it's also about recognizing that on the other side of these emotions is a newfound sense of freedom— a freedom to live life on your own terms, without the weight of societal expectations or the need to conform.

Menopause as a Time of Rebirth

In many ways, menopause can be seen as a time of rebirth—a shedding of the old to make way for the new. Just as a butterfly must leave behind its cocoon to fully emerge, so too must we let go of the old versions of ourselves to step into the women we are becoming. This shedding is not always easy. It requires courage to release the identities, roles, and expectations that have defined us for so long. But in doing so, we create space for something new to emerge.

For some women, this period of life is a time of rediscovery. Freed from the pressures of raising children or building a career, there is now an opportunity to explore passions that may have been put on hold. Whether it's pursuing a creative hobby, traveling, starting a new business, or engaging in community work, menopause can be a time of incredible personal growth and fulfillment.

This is also a time to reconnect with your purpose. What lights you up? What brings you joy? What legacy do you want to leave behind? Menopause invites us to ask these questions and to live our lives with greater intention and authenticity. It's a chance to define success on your own terms, to pursue what makes you truly happy, and to live in alignment with your deepest values.

The Power of Self-Love

At the heart of redefining menopause is the practice of self-love. This is a time when the world may try to tell you that you are losing your value—that youth, beauty, and vitality are slipping away—self-love reminds us that our worth is not determined by the external, by the way we look, or by the roles we play. Our worth is inherent, and it only grows as we age.

Self-love during menopause means caring for yourself in the way that you would care for a dear friend. It means speaking to yourself with kindness, listening to your body with compassion, and honoring your needs without guilt. It's about setting boundaries, saying no when you need to, and giving yourself permission to rest. It's about nourishing yourself—mind, body, and soul—so that you can move through this transition feeling supported, cared for, and loved.

This is also a time to cultivate gratitude for the body that has carried you through so much. While menopause may bring physical challenges, it's also a reminder of the incredible strength and resilience of the female body. Your body has carried you through decades of life, through joy and pain, through growth and change. It has adapted, healed, and supported you in countless ways. Now, as it undergoes yet another transformation, it deserves your deepest love and care. Rather than focusing on the discomforts or frustrations that menopause may bring, shift your focus to gratitude. Thank your body for all it has done and continues to do for you. Celebrate the wisdom and experience it holds, and recognize that every change is a testament to its strength.

Moving Through Menopause with Grace

One of the most powerful ways to navigate menopause is to move through it with grace. Grace, in this context, is not about perfection or composure. It's about being gentle with yourself and allowing yourself to move through this transition with kindness, patience, and acceptance. Grace means letting go of the need to "get it right" and trusting that you are doing the best you can with the knowledge and resources you have.

Moving through menopause with grace also means embracing flexibility. As your body changes, so too will your needs. What worked for you in your 30s and 40s may no longer serve you in your 50s and beyond. Be willing to adapt, to try new things, and to explore different ways of caring for yourself. Whether it's finding new forms of exercise, experimenting with alternative therapies, or adjusting your diet, give yourself permission to explore what feels good for you at this stage of life.

Another key aspect of grace is forgiveness—especially self-forgiveness. Menopause can bring up a lot of emotions, and it's easy to fall into the trap of self-criticism. You may feel frustrated with your body, overwhelmed by the changes, or discouraged by the physical symptoms. But grace invites you to forgive yourself for those feelings. It encourages you to release the guilt, the frustration, and the expectation that you should be handling everything perfectly. Grace is about accepting that you are human, that you are learning, and that it's okay to struggle sometimes.

Cultivating Community and Connection

One of the most important things to remember during menopause is that you are not alone. Every woman goes through this journey, and there is incredible power in connecting with others who are navigating the same transition. Menopause can feel isolating at times, especially if you don't have people in your life who understand what you're going through. But seeking out a supportive community—whether that's through friends, family, or online groups—can make all the difference.

There is something deeply healing about sharing your experiences with other women who understand. It's in these connections that you can find comfort, validation, and support. You can share tips, exchange stories, and remind each other that you are not alone in this journey. Surrounding yourself with a community of women who are also embracing menopause with grace and positivity can help you feel empowered and supported.

It's also worth noting that the more we talk about menopause openly, the more we can dismantle the stigma and silence that often surrounds it. Menopause is a natural part of life, and yet it is often treated as something shameful or embarrassing. By sharing your experiences and encouraging others to do the same, you contribute to a culture where menopause is seen as a normal, beautiful, and powerful transition. You create space for honest conversations and help other women feel seen and understood.

Redefining Beauty and Aging

One of the biggest cultural challenges women face during menopause is the pervasive narrative that aging is something to be feared, fought, or avoided. Society places so much value on youth that women are often made to feel invisible or irrelevant as they age. But menopause offers an opportunity to redefine what beauty and aging mean to us on a personal level.

True beauty is not defined by wrinkle-free skin, a youthful figure, or external appearances. It is defined by confidence, wisdom, and authenticity. As we move through menopause, we have the chance to embrace a new kind of beauty—one that comes from within. It's the beauty of a woman who knows herself, who has lived, who has loved, and who carries the wisdom of her experiences with pride.

Aging is not something to resist; it is something to honor. Every line, every change in our bodies, is a reflection of the life we have lived. These changes are not signs of decline but of resilience, strength, and growth. When we shift our perspective on aging, we can begin to see menopause as a time to embrace ourselves fully, without the need to conform to society's narrow standards of beauty.

Honoring the Spiritual Journey of Menopause

For many women, menopause is not just a physical or emotional transition, but a deeply spiritual one. It is a time of profound introspection, reflection, and awakening. As the body releases its reproductive role, there is often a sense of stepping into a new phase of life—one that is more aligned with personal truth, purpose, and authenticity.

This spiritual aspect of menopause invites us to connect with ourselves on a deeper level. It is an opportunity to ask the big questions: Who am I now? What do I want to do with the rest of my life? What is my purpose? Menopause can be a catalyst for spiritual growth, guiding us to explore our inner world and align our outer lives with our inner truths.

Many women find that menopause is a time when they become more attuned to their intuition, their inner wisdom, and their connection to something greater than themselves. This may be a time to explore practices that support your spiritual journey, whether that's meditation, journaling, spending time in nature, or engaging in creative expression. These practices can help you stay grounded, centered, and connected to the deeper meaning of this transition.

Embracing the Wisdom Years

As we move through menopause, we step into what is often called "the wisdom years"—a time when we are no longer defined by the roles of motherhood, career, or societal expectations, but by the depth of our experience and the strength of our inner selves. These years are a time to fully embrace who we are, without apology or explanation.

The wisdom years are not about retreating from life; they are about stepping into it with more clarity, purpose, and joy than ever before. This is a time to celebrate all that you have learned, all that you have overcome, and all that you have yet to experience. It is a time to live boldly, to pursue your passions, and to give yourself permission to enjoy life fully.

Menopause, in this light, becomes not just a biological event, but a spiritual awakening. It is a time when the external roles and responsibilities begin to fall away, allowing us to connect with our true essence. It is a time to honor the wisdom we have gained, to trust in the journey, and to embrace the fullness of who we are becoming.

A Journey of Grace, Strength, and Self-Love

Menopause is a sacred journey—one that deserves to be honored, celebrated, and embraced with grace. It is a time of transformation, growth, and rebirth. While it may bring challenges, it also offers us the opportunity to reconnect with ourselves, to redefine beauty and aging, and to step into a deeper, more authentic version of who we are.

As we move through this journey, let us do so with compassion for ourselves, gratitude for our bodies, and a sense of curiosity and wonder for what lies ahead. Let us trust the process, knowing that we are not alone and that every step of this journey is leading us toward greater wisdom, strength, and joy.

Above all, let us remember that menopause is not an ending, but a beginning—a new chapter in the story of our lives, filled with possibility, growth, and the freedom to live life on our own terms. This is the time to love ourselves more deeply than ever before, to honor the changes in our bodies and our lives, and to embrace this transformation with grace, strength, and self-love.

Sylvia Becker-Hill

Founder of Becker-Hill Inc.

https://www.linkedin.com/in/sylviabeckerhill/
https://www.facebook.com/SylviaBeckerHillBiz
https://www.instagram.com/sylviabeckerhill/
https://becker-hill.com/
https://talkwithsylvia.com/

Sylvia Becker-Hill is a true Renaissance woman, a 9-times published bestselling author, and a seasoned edutainer who has empowered thousands of corporate executives, women leaders, and entrepreneurs around the world since 1997.

In 2002, she became the first German coach to earn the coveted title of Professional Certified Coach from the International Coach Federation, establishing herself as an industry-shaping pioneer in the coaching world.

Her impressive educational background boasts two university degrees, while her portfolio showcases over 30 certifications in various change modalities, including her accreditation as one of the world's first 10 Certified Master Neuroplasticians in 2023.

Sylvia's mission is to empower you with all the knowledge, tools, and lasting transformation you need to "FLIP" everything that bothers, hurts, or blocks you from living your dream life into unquestionable Freedom, unconditional Love, envisioned Identity, and impactful Power.

Are you ready to feel unabashedly alive and powerful?

FLIP Unwanted Changes into Milestones of Empowerment

By Sylvia Becker-Hill

Menopause - A Time of Surprises

"Menopause felt like losing control and the death of my old self.
It was scary, lonely, painful, and exhausting.
But in the end, a wiser, stronger woman emerged,
like new flowers after a harsh winter."
—Sylvia Becker-Hill

Growing up in Germany in the late 60s/70s, my mother was the only woman I saw going through menopause. Her experience, as I remember it, can be summed up in five words: "Ten years of sweating hell." Sleepless nights, exhaustion, and the embarrassment of her once beautiful, curly blonde hair sticking flat to her sweaty neck and forehead became her new reality.

When menopause hit me, I had been living in the USA for 11 years, far from my mother, who was now struggling with dementia. I felt alone with this topic in a culture where intimate conversations like this weren't common. I was unprepared and shocked by how quickly it came.

Now, I'm going to share details that might feel like "TMI"—too much information—depending on your background, but I wish women in my life had shared openly with me. So, consider this an invitation to stay open-hearted. Every woman's menopause journey is unique—you may not experience my symptoms or struggles—but I hope my story will inspire and help you.

An important note: I'm not a women's health expert or a doctor. I'm a woman who faced menopause alone, struggling with health and sexual challenges and navigating the medical system to protect my body and find solutions that worked for me.

I also bring in my experience as a women's empowerment mentor, executive coach, and change management consultant of over 28 years. Even though this knowledge is professional and corporate, it empowered me as I navigated my own challenging journey.

At the end of this chapter, you'll find a QR code that links to a list of resources and products I endorse and use myself. It took me years to find the right products, and I wish someone had shared them with me earlier. It could have saved me many painful and frustrating days.

Blood Blood Blood

*"Expectations are usually a guarantee for disappointment
and harsh awakening."*
—Sylvia Becker-Hill

I expected perimenopause to bring irregular, lighter periods, eventually tapering off. Instead, it was the opposite. After decades of predictable, light periods every 28 days, I suddenly experienced heavy bleeding— soaking thick pads in 90 minutes—for weeks at a time, with only brief breaks.

This impacted my life daily. I wore only black pants due to frequent "blood accidents" and spent a fortune on the biggest pads available. Some days, blood would pool on my car seat, and my husband and I had to cover our mattress with plastic to avoid buying a new one every few weeks. Our sex life dwindled to once every 5 to 7 weeks during those few non-bleeding days over 1.5 years.

The heavy bleeding was exhausting, scary, embarrassing, and weakening. Doctors suspected cancer due to a fast-growing, grapefruit-sized fibroid in my uterus that couldn't be removed without a full hysterectomy. An MRI and painful biopsy confirmed it was benign, but five doctors— ranging from traditional to alternative—suggested either a hysterectomy or other invasive surgeries with potential complications.

None of these doctors admitted they didn't know the cause of the bleeding or how to stop it. Instead, they tried to "sell" their solutions, leaving me frustrated, especially with the female doctors who were blind to the male-centric healthcare system's impact on their style of caring.

Gratefully, I had the confidence to question authority. I sensed the doctors simply didn't know the answer, so I turned inward. It might sound crazy, but I started talking to my fibroid and uterus. Once I stopped chasing external answers and lay quietly with my hands on my belly, the stress evaporated. I wish I had done this sooner! My body reassured me: "I'm not dangerous," the fibroid said. "I just have a message for you." "I'm the seat of your creative power," my uterus said. "You need me."

Soon after, I read The Wisdom of Menopause by Christiane Northrup, M.D., where a sentence caught my eye: "Fibroids can often represent blocked creativity." It hit me. I finally pursued an old dream, signing a book contract. Forty days later, my first solo book became an international bestseller. Despite the continued heavy bleeding, I no longer felt fear.

During a visit to Germany, I remembered a homeopathic doctor who had helped me years before. I saw her, and five days after taking tiny sugar pills filled with "information" and not pharmaceuticals, the heavy bleeding stopped and never returned. The fibroid started shrinking, and though it remains, I am symptom-free and get it measured once a year through a harmless ultra-sound.

Disclaimer: I'm not a medical professional and am not advising against hysterectomies. I'm simply sharing my personal story and decisions.

The point is: Consult multiple professionals, listen to your body, and trust your intuition. Use all the information to decide what's right for you. Only you can know that.

Fibroids and Women's Creativity

"When I don't create I become spiritually constipated."
—Sylvia Becker-Hill

Many women, myself included, rediscover their creativity in their forties or later. Sadly, life's demands—school, work, marriage, family—can suppress our innate creativity instead of nurturing it. Yet, creativity is the divine spark of our soul!

It doesn't matter what form it takes—painting, photography, gardening, crocheting. The key is finding that sweet spot where your skills are just challenged enough and passion and interest are high to keep you learning and growing. Flow states become possible, making you lose track of time and self, and your inner critic's voice quietens. Creativity becomes not just fun but healing, sparking powerful self-healing processes in the brain, body, and, I believe, the soul.

Rumors and Reality

"The menopause experience is as unique as every woman is.
Set clear boundaries in your mind and with others who try to tell you
otherwise!
You do you—that goes for menopause like for everything else in your life.
Talking with other women is encouraged, but comparison is forbidden.
The first creates connection and support;
the latter causes heartache and can cost you friendships."
—Sylvia Becker-Hill

Moving from Michigan to California in my late forties was a bigger culture shock than moving from Germany to Michigan. In some ways, California made life easier for my outspoken nature; in others, it became even more "hustling and bustling." But I loved how women were more open about intimate experiences. I'll never forget a business networking meeting where a woman introduced herself as a "post-divorce women's sexuality empowerment mentor." I admired her boldness, and we became networking buddies.

Unfortunately, I made a mistake: I compared my menopause experience to hers. She bragged about newfound sexual freedom and multiple orgasms, while my reality was much different.

I had always been a sensual, easily aroused woman, physically and mentally. My body was always ready for intimacy—until menopause hit. Suddenly, I felt like a desert—dried out and completely devoid of libido. It was a shock. No one had prepared me for this.

I didn't have hot flashes or brain fog. Instead, I dealt with a complete loss of libido and painful vaginal dryness. Walking in underwear became uncomfortable. There were no star-dancing orgasms or cascading multiples—just emptiness. And after battling doctors to preserve my uterus, I had no professional locally to talk to. When COVID hit, I lost my in-person women's circles, and my professional Zoom calls didn't feel like the place to discuss vaginal dryness.

It was a lonely, horrible phase of menopause. Things improved when I finally opened up to my husband and close girlfriends. Now, my libido has returned, though not as strong as before. I credit time, hormonal changes, supplements like Omega-3 fish oil, yoni steaming, and finding the right oils and creams. (You can find the products I use on my downloadable resource list.)

Menopause and Marriage

"I was blessed with a gentle, caring husband.
Looking back, I would start sharing my fears and worries earlier.
Protecting his peace of mind was my childhood coping mechanism of
'people pleasing,' instead of asking for what I needed right from the start."
—Sylvia Becker-Hill

Not every woman has a supportive partner during menopause. My husband accepted without complaint that, for about three years, we had little to no sex. He was sweet, caring, and never showed discomfort during my "bloody waterfall phase." He patiently cleaned my car seat, changed our bed, carried out overflowing waste bins, and protected our mattress with plastic sheets.

Menopause can put pressure on marriages, leading to misunderstandings. Don't let that happen! Talk to your partner early, as soon as you sense perimenopause starting. Share your fears and needs, and release any shame. Over half of humanity goes through this, and the other half needs us to inform them.

How to FLIP Unwanted Changes into Milestones of Empowerment

"I can now see a future with a different culture!
One where we women prepare to embrace the scary changes and turn
them into milestones of empowerment, celebrating them together."
—Sylvia Becker-Hill

Mindset and Attitude Tips:

1. Death and aging are part of life—accept this truth.

2. If you have a female body, you will go through menopause. Embrace it without resistance, as resistance only makes the process harder.

3. Everything changes, including ourselves.

4. Let go of any expectations about how your menopause will unfold, when it will start, how long it will last, and when it will end. Embrace the unknown as a neutral fact.

5. Journal about your beliefs on aging and menopause. Read them slowly and notice how each belief feels in your body. Ask yourself:

   - Does this belief serve your highest well-being?

- Does it feel aligned in your body?
- Is it aligned with how you want to feel about your sensuality as a woman?

If your answer is yes to all three questions, keep the belief. If no, focus on the sensation the belief caused. Stay with it, even if it's uncomfortable until it dissipates. Use curiosity and compassion to let it go.

6. Create new beliefs that align with your vision of how you want to move through menopause. Read them aloud, sense how your body reacts, and adjust until you joyfully embody them.

Research Tips:

1. Research, research, research!

2. Google or ChatGPT can answer any question. When using ChatGPT, always ask for sources.

3. Join online forums or local women's groups that match your interests, values, and style.

Communication Tips:

1. Release your fear of judgment. You *will* be judged—it's human nature. The key is not to take it personally. Expect it, normalize it, and let it no longer stop you from speaking your truth.

2. Interview the women in your family, especially your mother, about their experiences with aging and menopause. Just listen—don't judge or compare.

3. Expand these conversations to women outside your family.

4. Use these talks to become aware of any fears or beliefs you're holding. Release them through movement or somatic therapy.

5. Share your fears with other women to release them, not to wallow in them.

6. Ask more questions about menopause, especially to your healthcare providers before changes begin.

7. If you have a partner, share your journey with them. Include them in your research, and ask if they have any questions or concerns. Tell them what you need, but recognize their boundaries. You are responsible for fulfilling your needs, and if your partner helps, see it as a gift, not an obligation.

8. If menopause affects your work performance, talk to your boss about your needs. If you're self-employed, consider scaling back your business to make room for the changes ahead. Plan your communication strategy in advance.

Self-Care Tips:

1. Make self-care a joyful expression of love for yourself and your body.

2. Prioritize quality sleep—treat it as your most precious resource.

3. Clean your sheets every two weeks and invest in silk or high-quality cotton ones.

4. Invest in a scale that measures your body's water percentage, and drink enough to keep it above 50%.

5. Move daily, even if it's just gentle stretching or a short walk.

6. Take breaks every 90 minutes, and consider using a standing desk with varying heights for different postures.

7. Get a yearly gynecological check-up with hormone testing.

8. Pamper yourself with a weekly yoni steam bath.

9. Care for your genitals with skin-nurturing oils each night.

10. Give yourself lymphatic massages three times a week.

11. Create a sacred space with an altar, candle, flowers, and meditation pillow.

12. Stretch on a yoga mat twice daily, morning and evening, for 10 minutes.

13. Spend an hour weekly in green nature and leave your phone in your car!

14. Avoid stress as much as possible.

15. Rest, rest, and rest more.

16. Fill your life with laughter and intimate conversations with friends.

17. Read more, watch less TV.

18. Enjoy board games and puzzles with loved ones.

19. Keep a journal by your bed and take it with you when you travel.

20. Experiment with genital toys like yoni balls or clitoris stimulators.

21. Treat yourself to beautiful boudoir coffee table books.

22. Consider booking a boudoir photo shoot. Frame and hang your favorite photos in your bedroom as a celebration of yourself.

(My vetted and recommended self-care products are available on my downloadable list here: www.becker-hill.com/selfcareproducts.)

A Rising Tide Lifts All Boats

"I believe in a world where women's bodies are revered—where menstruation, hormones, masturbation, and menopause are openly discussed without shame.
A world where daughters grow up cherished, informed, and protected, with rituals that honor every stage of a woman's life."
—Sylvia Becker-Hill

I dream of a society where our experiences are shared without judgment but with respect, empathy, and laughter from joy, not shame. I know this world is possible because I've seen it on a small scale, where a dozen women and I created it together. If we can do it, it means it's possible. Now, it's time for more courageous women to step up and follow our example.

One day, our small waves will merge into a tsunami, catapulting the world into a new era of empowered womanhood. Maybe you're one of those "authenticity warrioresses," joining me and others in your own unique way. The world is waiting for us.

Wise post-menopausal women will be the leaders of tomorrow, bringing peace and solving global challenges. Why? Because we are the **champions of change**, equipped with **the skills and compassion the world needs** to navigate the crises ahead.

Perhaps we'll meet one day at a conference celebrating this new era, dancing the night away in joy. Maybe that day is sooner than we think...

xoxo,

Sylvia

Heather Hanson

Flourish Nutritional Therapy Consultant
Gut-Brain Synergy Coach

https://www.linkedin.com/in/heather-hanson-870752b1/
https://www.facebook.com/flourishntp
https://www.instagram.com/flourishnutritionaltherapy/
https://flourishnutritionaltherapy.com/

Heather Hanson, affectionately known as the "Gut Health Paramedic," is the visionary behind the transformative Digestive CPR Framework. As a wellness expert, she's on a mission to empower business leaders and entrepreneurs to conquer the relentless issues of bloating, fatigue, brain fog, and weight gain that the medical community often leaves unresolved.

Heather's proprietary methods focus on digestive health, hormone balance, detoxification, and powerful mindset shifts. By healing the body at a cellular level—from the inside out—she enables individuals to transition from simply surviving to truly thriving, freeing them to live lives full of passion and purpose without the constant worry and wonder. This holistic approach empowers clients to unlock their true potential, achieve their career goals, and embrace self-love along the journey.

With an impressive 26-year career in healthcare, Heather intimately understands the struggles her clients face. Her journey is deeply personal, having triumphed over autoimmune thyroid disease using her groundbreaking methodologies. Now, she shares her insights and expertise to help others achieve unparalleled wellness and vitality.

Defying the Menopause Myths: My Journey to Wellness and Success

By Heather Hanson

"Just the Word Menopause Is Enough to Make a Person Cringe"

Menopause. UGH! The thought of losing my vibrance and becoming an old lady with wrinkles is something that I never thought would happen, at least not at the age of 47, when I thought I was in the prime of my life. I created my dream practice, was my own boss, and had aspirations of creating a wellness empire. I had all of these titles: wife, mother, nana, entrepreneur, CEO, dog mom, and adventure junky. I was very proud of all of them. I was on top of the world!

Then, in the blink of an eye, I was punched in the gut. MENOPAUSE! The social stigma around it is enough to make a person cringe. I can hear it now: "Your best years are behind you." "You've lost the glow of your youth." "You are outdated and replaceable." "Younger is better." If you are reading this, I am sure you get these feelings.

I will never forget the emptiness and sadness I felt as I stared at my lab results. It sure looked like I was in menopause. My FSH was sky-high, and for the first time ever, my estrogen was under 18. Normally, even with just one ovary, my estrogen was in the 300s. My last real period was back in 2000, right before a surprising hysterectomy at age 25. I went in to get a dermoid tumor and an ovary removed, but woke up with a big incision from hip to hip and was told they also took out my uterus because of severe endometriosis. But, that's a story for another time. It took me eight years, a lot of stubbornness, a gluten/dairy-free diet, and unintentional trauma healing to finally get my hormones balanced, and I wasn't ready to lose that so quickly. My one ovary was doing a great job, and then BAM!

Deep down, I knew it was true. I was in menopause. My face looked like it was melting off, my belly had a pooch, sleep was worse than ever, I was waking up feeling on fire, my sex drive was nonexistent, I was irritable, to say the least, had difficulty concentrating, my energy felt like someone sucked the life out of me, and to top it off, my hair was thinning. I had long, thick, healthy red hair, and now it looked frail, lackluster, and dry. I felt deflated and like I was melting into a pile of goo.

I wasn't ready to accept menopause symptoms as my fate for the rest of my life, so I decided to use my holistic health background and find the best person I could to help me. I wanted to enter into this next phase of life with energy, grace, calmness, and strength and not let this death sentence of menopause define how I was going to live the rest of my life. I am WAY too stubborn for that.

"Why Isn't Anyone Listening to Me"

Having a background in nursing, I tend to choose to work with nurse practitioners. I did some research, picked "the perfect person," and waited five months for the appointment. It was 2021, so getting an in-person appointment was still difficult. The exam room was devoid of any warmth or character. The nurses and admin staff were distant and almost robotic. It was an eerie feeling. When the NP entered the room, she spent 90 seconds asking the standard questions. I described my symptoms, knowing that she would have a solution for me. Unfortunately, her response was that I was a little young to be in menopause, the transition was normal, and there was no need to repeat blood work or start on estrogen. I was speechless and taken aback by the lack of care and compassion! Did she not hear all of my complaints? I had a laundry list: hot flashes, night sweats, weight gain, thinning hair, dry skin, irritability, insomnia, and did I mention irritability?

I left that appointment upset and frustrated. I desperately wanted someone to listen to me. To help me. To guide me. I wanted someone to have my back. I wanted to be treated like I treat my clients. I wanted connection, hope, and a plan. Instead, I left feeling lost and alone.

"Am I Ever Going to Feel Like Myself Again"

Nine months later, my symptoms were worse and dragging me down a dusky path. The hot flashes were more frequent and lasted longer. Brain fog was robbing me of my photographic memory. This made it feel like I was trudging through the mud, every day. It was interfering with my work significantly and I felt like I was losing myself. I was known for my laughter. When I worked in an office, everyone heard it. People could always find me from my loud laugh. Now, I could not remember the last time I laughed.

Well. People were struggling. Past traumas kept bubbling up for me, as well as my clients. I am really good at handling stress, although, this felt different. I felt like I had the weight of the world on my shoulders, and I could barely take a step forward. There is no doubt that 2020 brought on so many challenges for my family and my clients. All of the root-cause processes that I take my clients through were not working as I remember sitting at my desk wondering if I was ever going to feel like myself again. I felt hollow and sad for no reason. I decided to try again to find help. I made an appointment with an integrative, holistic nurse practitioner. Surely, she would listen, right!? This appointment was booked three months out. I made a list of my symptoms: fatigue, weight gain, disrupted sleep, hot flashes, hair loss, saggy and crepey skin, sadness, irritability…

"Man, I Feel Awesome! I Love This"

The day came for the appointment, which made me incredibly nervous. "Was she going to listen?" She agreed to do advanced blood work to make sure the auto-immune thyroiditis was still under control and discuss hormone replacement, although she required a mammogram first. Great! More waiting... I made an appointment for the mammogram, three more months out. Finally, I felt that there was hope on the horizon. Through this appointment and deep mindset work in a transformational mindset facilitation certification program, I found hope and the reassurance that I would soon feel like myself again.

In April 2023, I started estradiol and testosterone (I also continued the compounded progesterone that I had been on since 2014). One week in, and I felt amazing. I kept thinking this is too good to be true!! I felt good...better than good...I felt great! I felt happy...my brain was on fire and so clear...my energy was pumping. I felt like the estrogen was my crack. Seriously, a drug... I felt so good that I was afraid to miss a dose. I remember driving home one day thinking, "Man, I feel awesome! I love this."

"Desire Minus Resistance = Desired Outcome"

On my 49th birthday, I made a decision that menopause was not going to define me. It was not going to own me. Tell me that I should just get used to feeling this way and that I was just getting old. I made a firm decision and commitment to myself that I was going to be the fittest, healthiest, happiest, most content, and most successful in my career by my 50th birthday, and I was going to do this without being on a crazy diet or workout plan and without being in hustle and grind. This decision was certain, I could see myself doing it, and nothing or no one was going to get in my way. As my mentor David Bayer says, "Desire minus resistance = desired outcome." See yourself living your desire, without knowing the how, then taking action toward the goal.

Later that month, I embarked on one of the most transformative journeys of my life at a mindset retreat in Costa Rica with my business coaching group. At the opening meet and greet, we were asked to set our intentions for the weekend. At this point, I thought that all of the struggles that I went through in my life made me who I am and that I did not have resentments. Came to find out, I had resentments and lots of them. The main resentment I uncovered was that my mother did not keep me safe, which led me to have a core program of control.

This core programming served me for years and helped me become a strong, independent woman, who did not let anyone tell her that she could not accomplish something she wanted. On the other hand, this need to control my environment also created havoc in my life. I developed severe body image issues and an eating disorder at the age of 15 and carried it with me through the next 25 years of my life. To be honest, I still struggled with this until last year.

The control did not stop there. I controlled everything and anything I could, which led to over-exercising, over-working, codependency…overdoing for others, so that I could feel good about myself. I needed to be busy doing something at all times, so that I did not have to deal with all of the noise that I shoved down, deep inside. Even though I showed up strong and confident to other people, inside, I constantly slung crap at myself. Not good enough, pretty enough, worthy enough, educated enough… I told myself such ugly things. Things that I would never say to anyone else.

What I realized through the process was that I was never in control to begin with, and the things most out of my control were the things that shaped my life and created tremendous growth.

"I Wanted Something More"

November 2024: I had been looking forward to a large women's networking conference for months. To say that I was excited is an understatement. 12,000 women from all over would be in attendance. It was a dreary, rainy day, which caused major traffic backups leading me to be two hours behind schedule, although that did not quell my excitement. I parked, took a brisk one-mile walk to the conference hall, and found my table, just in time for the first speaker to start. It was a great talk, although I felt the excitement waning. Three more rounds of speakers later, I found myself wanting to be anywhere except that convention center. I felt bored and disappointed. I left early, which is something that I have never done. As I walked to my car, so many thoughts swirled through my head. I left the conference early. Hours early, but why? The speakers were top-notch. They had great things to say.

It was on my drive home that it hit me. This conference was for 20, 30, and 40-year-olds and here I was, one of the oldest people in the room. I had just spent the last nine months deep-diving into mindset work and did not want to be in a place that just scratched the surface. I had done the work and wanted something more.

I came to the conclusion that women need to define who they are within each decade of their lives.

My 40s have been so packed full of life-changing events. I left my job of 14 years for my "dream job," which actually turned out to be a nightmare, although I met the most amazing people. My youngest child graduated, I became a nana, started a functional medicine practice from the ground up, then left two years later to pursue my own practice, moved from my home of 18 years, lived apart from my husband for 22 months due to a work transfer (although it was like we were dating again), 2020 happened, my husband retired, I was in the process of revamping my practice to truly get another layer deeper into the root cause.

I was now in my 50th year of life. There is so much life to live. So much joy to be had. I was going to fulfill the promises I made to myself on my 49th birthday.

"You Are Not Just Getting Old"

No one can tell you that you are just getting old and need to accept and manage symptoms. You are not destined to have brain fog, bloating, and fatigue. You are not destined to gain weight because you are in perimenopause or postmenopause. My question to you: Who do you want to be, and how do you want to feel in this decade of life? If you are ready to take bold action and feel better, grab some water, your notebook, and maybe even a cup of coffee. It's time to dream a little bit. Don't worry about the how, just use your imagination like you did when you were a kid.

Open your notebook and write these questions down (feel free to change things up with questions that resonate with you more):

- What do I want out of this decade of my life?
- How do I want to feel when I wake up in the morning?
- What do I want my career to look like?
- Where do I want to travel?
- Who do I want to spend time with?

Take 15–30 minutes or so and dream, then journal about what you saw in your future.

"Your Diagnosis Is Not Your Destiny!"

Menopause is not a death sentence, and a diagnosis is not your destiny. It does not mean that you have reached your maximum potential. Whether you are going through perimenopause, menopause, or some other health challenge, it does not define you. There are actions you can take to feel the way you want to feel. The first step is making the decision to take action, so here are some tips to stay fit, healthy, and strong at any age and especially during menopause:

- Do something hard every day! I make my workouts hard.
- Lift weight and/or do resistance training. I do HIIT training with weights at F-45. This will help with not only building and maintaining muscle, it will also help keep your bones strong.
- Eat to nourish your body. Eat protein. Eat a rainbow. Don't be afraid of healthy fats. Eat carbs; your gut microbiome needs them to thrive and support you.
- Get sleep. Sleep is a necessity to help the body regenerate at the cellular level. Getting less sleep to do other things is not a badge of honor.
- Hydrate (balance water and mineral intake). Aim for half of your body weight in ounces of water, every day. Also, make sure you are getting enough minerals.
- Be kind to yourself. Women tend to sling ugly, nasty words at themselves. Things that they would never say to another person. "I need to lose weight." "I look old." "I am a mess."
- Don't sweat the small stuff. As my mentor, David Bayer, says, "The problem is not the problem. It's the thinking about a situation that is the problem."
- Get a coach. I have two. One for fitness and one for business, although I will tell you that my business coach uses 80% mindset coaching.
- Be in a community of like-minded individuals.
- Show thanks and gratitude daily.
- Show up in relationships as the person that you want to be in a relationship with. That energy exchange can create dynamic changes in a relationship.
- Your happiness is an inside job. No one else is responsible for your happiness.

Your best years are not behind you! I am loving my life at 50 more than I did in my 20s, 30s, and 40s. I've talked to some women in their 70s and 80s who feel that they have gotten better with age and love each decade in their life.

I know that this transition can be scary, but your life is just beginning, and there are so many amazing things coming your way! I choose to embrace aging and challenge myself to continually grow and pursue new things. I challenge you to do the same. Menopause does not have to hold you back, instead, it can be a catapult to new and exciting adventures.

Urszula Kudla

Founder of DiLove Wellness Studio Inc.
Wellness Mentor

https://www.linkedin.com/in/wellnessmamaliving
https://www.facebook.com/urszula.kudla
https://www.instagram.com/wellnessmamaliving
https://www.wellnessmamaliving.com
https://urszulakudla.com/

I'm Urszula, a dedicated self-care mentor, natural beauty advocate, and EFT practitioner. My mission is to empower women to discover the healer within themselves, enabling them to reach their highest potential and live fulfilling lives. With a focus on holistic health, I guide individuals toward optimal well-being in mind, body, and spirit through EFT tapping, journaling, meditation, and transformative retreats.

I am also passionate about creating supportive tools such as affirmation cards, journals, and digital books. These resources are designed to help individuals on their self-love journey, fostering a life of gratitude and positivity. My own path, marked by both challenges and victories, has ignited a deep desire to inspire and uplift others through my experiences.

I believe in the transformative impact of a healthy mindset, practicing empowering habits, self-care, and self-love.

I am committed to sharing my story and helping others manifest their best lives.

I Was Not a Victim of Menopause, But of My Lifestyle Choices

By Urszula Kudla

I recognize that the quality of my life is a direct reflection of the quality of my habits, and I am working on implementing positive habits each day.
—Urszula Kudla

It was well past midnight when I woke up feeling an intense heat. I was scared because I had just undergone two serious surgeries that year. I thought I might have a fever. My thoughts raced at the speed of light, imagining various scenarios while feeling like someone had put me in an oven.

Yes, an oven—that's it. The thermostat on the heating must have broken and kept the heat on, making the house unbearably hot. I woke up my husband, who grumbled but got up to check. He came back saying everything was working fine. I started to feel calmer as my temperature gradually returned to normal. I felt better. I tossed and turned a bit, wondering what it could have been. My husband suggested it was probably just a bad dream. Maybe he was right, I thought. Perhaps I dreamed I was in hell. I laughed to myself at the thought because I had long stopped believing in hell. And I fell asleep again.

We forgot about the incident because of our busy lives with kids, work, and responsibilities. Who has time to ponder nightmares? Nothing unusual happened for a few weeks, except that my period was late. I was 45 years old. I could be pregnant, so I decided to buy a pregnancy test to calm my racing thoughts. I know children are a blessing, but I already had three grown-up kids and didn't want to go back to changing diapers. The test reassured me, confirming I wasn't pregnant. So, why hadn't I gotten my period? That question pounded in my head constantly for days.

One night, I woke up feeling my bedding was wet. I turned on the light, waking my husband. My side of the bed looked like someone had been slaughtered. Many men would faint at such a sight, but not my husband. He got up, brought paper towels, helped me clean everything up, and led me to the shower. I washed, put on fresh, dry sheets, and went back to bed. I always had heavy periods, but never like this. I was exhausted but clean and dry, so I quickly fell asleep.

My period lasted longer than usual, but at that moment, it wasn't a cause for worry. Life went on. I noticed I became moodier. Things that didn't bother me before started to irritate me. I attributed it to the recent surgeries and closing my business, which I hated. It didn't occur to me that it could be the beginning of menopause. The topic of menopause was taboo when I was growing up. No wonder the symptoms I had didn't make me think of menopause. It didn't cross my mind that I could be going through it.

Until one winter night, when I felt very cold. I pulled the comforter over myself, but it didn't help. I woke my husband again and told him the heating must be broken because it was freezing. He said he didn't feel cold but got up to check, to calm me down. He came back saying everything was working fine, "as before," he added. And then I had an epiphany. I remembered a friend's story about her menopause symptoms, including temperature swings. But she was much older. I'm only 45! I had internal conversations, convincing myself I was too young for menopause. But the question of "if not menopause, then what?" kept bothering me.

The hot and cold flashes became more frequent. My periods were long and heavy. There were days I didn't leave the house because a pad wouldn't last more than an hour. When my period extended to three weeks, I decided it was time to see a doctor. I felt weak. I suspected low iron and other vitamin and mineral deficiencies—after all, I was bleeding like a soldier on the battlefield. The family doctor said it was too early for menopause and referred me for an ultrasound to check for fibroids. The tests showed no fibroids, and everything looked fine.

So, what was wrong? I asked for a referral to a gynecologist. The gynecologist, after an examination, said that even though it was a bit early, it was possible that I was entering a premenopausal stage. He said there was no cure; "you just have to go through it," and to alleviate symptoms, pills were necessary. He did not even offer any tests or suggestions for lifestyle changes; a pill was his solution.

I couldn't accept that suggestion. My intuition told me there must be other solutions. I'm not the type to take a pill at the first sign of pain. I told the doctor I needed to discuss it with my husband, and with tears in my eyes, I went home. I felt hopeless and blamed myself for never having been interested in the topic of menopause. But how could I be interested when the word menopause was completely foreign to me?

After talking with my husband, I decided to do my own research and delve into the topic of menopause. For the next several weeks, I surfed the internet, studied scientific papers, and read books on the subject, trying to understand why women have such severe symptoms during perimenopause and menopause. Many women experience hot flashes and health problems. I was curious about the cause. I couldn't believe that God created such a wonderful being and gave women such a surprise. I simply couldn't believe it. Menopause should be just another stage of life, I thought. One thing I knew for sure—menopause doesn't have to be the end of life or a tragedy. It can be a beautiful, new stage of life that we will experience as we plan it, and I was determined to make this new chapter of my life as easy and joyful as I could.

I have learned that the symptoms associated with menopause can pass quickly, last long, or not occur at all. I wondered why women experience it differently. Some sources mentioned hormonal imbalances—too few hormones, too many hormones. Hormones, hormones, hormones. This word appeared frequently in many articles and scientific papers. I decided to delve deeper into the subject of female hormones and why our hormones become imbalanced, causing women to have such varied experiences during perimenopause and menopause. The obvious conclusion was that our well-being is not solely due to the loss of hormones but mainly due to the improper functioning of these hormones.

So, the question arises—what causes our hormones to not work properly? What throws our hormones out of balance to the point that they can't maintain equilibrium?

My intuition told me that our lifestyle causes hormonal imbalances. God created humans as a perfect creation; I couldn't believe He made a mistake here. And time confirmed that I was right. When we reach middle age, the loss of some hormones is necessary, but then other hormones decrease or increase their levels to maintain balance— another word that appeared frequently in various scientific works and books: *balance.*

So, I started narrowing my search to find the cause of my hormonal imbalance. I wondered what caused my endocrine system to be unbalanced and not work properly. Further investigations led me to the following conclusions: Women who had very mild symptoms or no symptoms at all usually led quite healthy lifestyles.

I decided to follow this lead. I won't detail how hormones work—I don't fully understand it myself, and perhaps no one does. One thing is certain: just like in many other areas of life and health, balance must be maintained. If there is no balance, our body immediately lets us know because our natural state is health and well-being, even during menopause. Yes, the hormonal changes that occur during perimenopause and menopause can affect how we feel, but it is up to us how we deal with these symptoms, how we prepare for menopause, and whether we adapt our lifestyle to the needs of our body and soul.

I concluded that changes must occur on three levels: body, mind, and soul.

Self-care should be an essential part of our lives...

The truth is, I wish I had understood it earlier. Growing up, the concept of self-care was unfamiliar territory. It wasn't that it was intentionally kept from me; rather, it was simply unknown. Even though self-care hadn't been part of my routine, after learning how our body is impacted by a lack of proper self-care and external factors, I was determined to make a change. Over the past decade, I've developed and committed to a self-care program that has profoundly transformed my life. Today, in my 60s, I feel stronger, more vibrant, and more beautiful than ever before.

Perimenopause and Menopause Basics

Perimenopause is a natural phase of life. Your body is beautifully designed to wind down at a certain point, giving you a release from reproduction.

Menopause is the complete absence of menstrual bleeding for at least one year. The hormonal rollercoaster ride of perimenopause ends. It is the start of a new beginning and a journey along the road of life.

TAKE BACK YOUR POWER

It bothers me that culture and often doctors tell women they have no control over how they're feeling. They say that hormones run the show, rather than you controlling your hormones, and that menopause is a hopeless season, with feeling overweight, tired, and miserable being just part of the course. Additionally, they often tell women that the only way to feel better is to pop a pill—whether it be birth control pills, bioidentical hormones, or antidepressants—to manage the symptoms and ease discomfort, without explaining the long-term side effects.

But there is more you can do. There are lifestyle changes, supplementation protocols, and self-care rituals that can help you get at the root cause and find balance for all the hormones playing a role in your symptoms. You must become the CEO of your own health, and you can naturally restore balance to your hormones and your life. With foundational lifestyle habits, including proper nutrition, supplementation, movement, and self-care, we can reset our hormones, restore health, and transition into perimenopause and beyond with ease and grace and without debilitating symptoms or medication. This is what I did naturally.

Ideally, perimenopause and menopause should be a natural transition that sets us up for a brand-new phase in our lives. The best way to naturally support our body through midlife and menopause is by getting our body functioning effectively on a cellular level through our daily habits, aided every step of the way by:

- **Proper nutrition:** Eating food that works for you, nourishing your body with all of the nutrients it needs to thrive, will ensure that your body gets back into balance and stays there. Eliminating inflammatory, carb-heavy foods from your diet, like bread, sugar, and alcohol, as well as high-sugar fruits, can help lessen hot flashes!

- **Movement:** Incorporating regular movement that makes your body and soul happy will strengthen and support your muscles, improve mental focus, and reduce stress while supporting hormone balance.

- **Self-care rituals:** Finding ways to care for yourself, from the inside out, will not only help put your body back in balance but allow you to support everyone and everything else in your life better.

- **Supplementation:** If you are struggling with hormone imbalances, it can be difficult to get the key nutrients you need from food alone. That's where supplements come in.

I neglected self-care for so many years that it was time for a change, time to reinvent myself.

It took me around six months from the day I started reinventing myself to see improvements, and around a year to feel vibrant and almost free of menopausal "fireworks." Changing my lifestyle and designing my self-care program helped me enjoy my life, and I am sure you can do it too.

The three most important things, I believe, that helped me balance my hormones and speed up my healing were:

1. **Eliminating all toxic products from my life:** During my research, I learned that some products contain chemicals that can mimic estrogen. We should be aware of the "foreign" estrogens present in our environment: xenoestrogens and synthetics. These two are known as endocrine disruptors, and they bring chaos and destruction to our hormones and our bodies. They are both artificial. Xenoestrogens such as BPA, parabens, and phthalates are found in everything from your personal and beauty care products to shopping receipts. Synthetic estrogens are those produced by the pharmaceutical industry and are found in birth control pills and hormone therapy. These are so close in molecular structure to natural estrogen that they can compete with our hormones for estrogen receptors.

Excess estrogen has been piling up in our systems for years. Adding the fact that progesterone is the first hormone to decline, and we are increasing our estrogen level using products containing those "foreign" estrogens, no wonder our hormones are out of balance. ***Even though estrogen levels do fall significantly after the last period, it's the relationship between estrogen and progesterone that matters, not the individual level of each one (balance).*** More things need to be addressed, but I am not able to squeeze everything into one chapter.

I believe a lot of women are aware of toxins in food and pesticides because when I talk to them about a healthy lifestyle, they quickly interrupt me with the statement, "But I eat healthy, mostly organic." But they don't quite make the connection that when they're applying personal care products, they're feeding that to their bodies. Not everything gets to our bloodstream, of course; the molecules must be small enough to penetrate the skin. But here's the kicker: all those products, especially anti-aging products, creams, moisturizers, and serums, are designed to penetrate. They are designed with molecules that are supposed to go deeper into your skin to do whatever it is they do, and many of them contain ingredients that are basically penetrators that drive the other ingredients even deeper.

When you apply these products to your skin and they penetrate, they go straight to your bloodstream, and from your bloodstream, they get sent all throughout your body to your organs. Also, we should remember that our skin is the largest organ in our body, and it's also a fundamental part of our immune system. Our skin's job is to keep us safe, and it does so constantly. So, when it's taxed like that, when we're feeding it these toxins, these synthetics, and all these ingredients, it's a double problem because we're putting these toxic ingredients inside our body, which disturb our hormones.

And we're also compromising our immune system.

Also, using cleaning products with toxic ingredients has a damaging impact on our bodies. We breathe in these chemicals all day long—from wearing clothes washed in harsh detergents and dried with dryer sheets to inhaling air fresheners. We also ingest these toxins from our plates and glasses, which retain chemical residues.

On average, a woman uses 15 personal care and cleaning products a day, which means she is exposing her body to around 200 different chemicals daily. I replaced all my personal care and cleaning products with plant-based alternatives free from harmful ingredients. Believe me, it was not easy to find those products 16 years ago, but I was desperate to improve my health and life. Nowadays, you can easily buy "clean" products, so it won't be difficult.

2. **Reducing stress, healing childhood trauma, and learning relaxation methods:** During my research, I learned that stress, especially chronic stress, is a major factor in elevating cortisol levels. If left unchecked, high cortisol throws off your estrogen, progesterone, and thyroid hormones. High cortisol results in feelings of overwhelm and worry and is closely linked to depression. Eliminating stress took me a little longer than I thought it would because I had to learn how to do it, and I found a lot of triggers from my childhood traumas.

Prioritizing self-care and other lifestyle changes to relieve your stress burden now and long term is one of the most powerful ways to improve your emotional well-being, and it can immediately make a difference in your life. I started to use essential oils, learned to meditate daily, and applied EFT (emotional freedom tapping) to release trauma and stress from my body. I worked with mentors and later decided to get my certificates to help others with similar problems. You may not even remember the trauma clearly at all, but the body remembers, and to journey with more ease and grace through menopause, you must address and heal past traumas. Everything is stored in our bodies; each of our cells has memories. I know that's easy to say and not so easy to do, but I want you to know that there are many effective ways of treating trauma and easing stress. For me, the most effective were EFT, meditations, acupuncture, and essential oils.

Also, I can't stress enough how important it is to do a detailed assessment of yourself before you start reinventing yourself. When you do an honest assessment, it will be easier to plan the necessary changes and tasks you need to make impactful changes.

3. **Changing my relationship with food:** As Hippocrates said, "Let food be thy medicine, and let medicine be thy food." High-quality nourishment is essential for well-being. I stopped eating highly processed and inflammatory foods, eliminated carbs and sugar, cut off alcohol consumption, and stopped eating out. Most of my meals were made from scratch. When I had to travel, I had a list of foods I could eat and always asked the restaurant staff if the kitchen could prepare something for me from this list if I couldn't find anything suitable on the menu. I never encountered any problems. I set up a food journal to note what I ate and marked down if I did not feel good after eating something. This allowed me to design my weekly meals later.

Gut health was and still is my priority. When I implemented those changes, I saw a difference not only in my body but also felt that my mind fogs were gone. Proper hydration was also my priority, and I started to make structured water for myself. All these changes made a huge impact on my menopause effects. It sounds like a lot, but believe me, once you make a plan, it is not difficult at all—maybe even easier—because you cook simpler.

My Advice

Design your personal self-care program that includes lifestyle changes necessary to heal your body, mind, and spirit:

- **Body:** Start with the detox, stop bombarding it with toxins, eat healthy and simple food, exercise, massage, and express love to your body daily.
- **Mind:** Reduce stress, practice daily positive affirmations, stop watching the news, and avoid participating in other people's drama.
- **Spirit:** Meditate daily, pray, and connect with nature often.

"Embrace self-care as a lifelong journey rather than a one-time fix. Every small step is progress."
—Urszula Kudla

How to Express Love to Your Body

1. Take a teaspoon of moringa oil (you can also use jojoba, almond, coconut, or any of your favorite carrier oils).

2. Add 5 drops of essential oil of your choice: lavender, ylang ylang, clary sage, frankincense.

3. After your shower, apply the mixture to your body and speak words of love and appreciation. Thank your legs for taking you around, your hands for doing everything that needs to be done, your tummy, your breasts, your hips, etc. Make this a daily habit.

4. If you don't have essential oils, you can use a good-quality moisturizer.

The point is to talk to your body with love and gratitude.

A free assessment form is available to download on my website. www.myassessment.ca or scan the QR code below.

Nicole Cabrias

Founder of Nicole Cabrias Coaching

https://www.linkedin.com/in/nicolecabrias/
https://www.facebook.com/passionrangerventures
https://www.instagram.com/nicolecabriascoaching/
https://nicolecabrias.com
https://menopowerproject.com

Nicole Cabrias is a Certified Personal Fitness Trainer, Nutrition Coach, Women's & Menopause Fitness Specialist and Life Coach Practitioner.

Now firmly in her 50s, Nicole has decided she's no longer interested in aging gracefully. Her plan is to Age Awesomely. And her mission is to help as many other women as possible do that too.

After decades abroad, and basically starting life over again at 43, Nicole decided to dust off her coaching credentials and figured out how to help women just like herself to not just survive, but actually thrive through the circus of physical, mental, emotional and major life changes that midlife and menopause brings.

Her refreshingly doable approach to exercise, eating and radical self care is based on the fact she believes it's totally possible to take back your body, look and feel amazing AND still enjoy the crap out of life too.

Secret Weapon of Choice: Redefining Fitness for Menopause and Aging Awesomely

By Nicole Cabrias

I was well into the weekly Zoom call with my business coach when the hot flash hit. Out of nowhere. Like a volcano suddenly erupted in the core of my soul. I was on fire, and I was oozing hot molten lava from the inside out. If you know the feeling, you *know*.

We were at that height of the on-again-off-again global pandemic lockdowns and social distancing, and I, along with every other fitness professional on the planet, was trying to figure out how to take my personal training and coaching techniques and make it all work online.

Somewhere from the depths of me peeling off layers, fanning furiously and mortified by the cooked lobster-looking person that was reflected back at me on the screen from my webcam, I could hear her saying, "You know, you're kind of in the perfect position to go all-in and niche down as a fitness specialist for women transitioning through and in menopause."

On so many levels, that made perfect sense. Working with other women in their forties, fifties and up was already my happy place. However, I resisted promoting the menopause angle. BIG TIME.

For whatever reason, the voice of Brad Pitt's character, in a movie I barely remembered from 1999, suddenly sprang to mind.

"The first rule of Fight Club is: you do not talk about Fight Club."

"I can't just focus on MENOPAUSE!" I whined to my coach. "Because... you know... that's TABOO!"

"The second rule of Fight Club is: you DO NOT talk about Fight Club!"

"What will people THINK? Menopause just isn't something you TALK ABOUT!!!" This went on for weeks as my hot-flash-fueled protests continued.

I was already creating my own fitness framework for this stage of life that I and my clients were seeing great success with. More importantly, we were feeling good and actually enjoying it. I also knew that these steps I was taking, and teaching, were significantly helping improve my own bizarre laundry list of menopausal symptoms. My clients were reporting similar things.

Menopause can feel like a full contact and very extreme sport. My personal experience with it certainly has been. And the heart of the problem we midlife and menopausal women face in navigating it with our sanity, our confidence, and our waistlines intact, is that it's not talked about openly, honestly, or anywhere near enough.

As women, we'll spend up to 40% of our lives in our menopause years. Yet, most of us slam into it uninformed and unprepared for what kinds of crazy things we might expect, or that there's much of anything we can do about it. I, for one, had been clueless.

That's not only ridiculous. It's totally unnecessary.

The irony of my reluctance to embrace the dreaded M word finally broke through. Menopause shouldn't be a secret one-woman fight club.

"Third rule of Fight Club: someone yells "stop!", goes limp, taps out, the fight is over."

That's the real punch to the gut, isn't it? We can scream and plead for it to stop. We can go limp and desperately wish we could tap out, but this is one fight that is never, ever going to be over. Some symptoms fade, others will mysteriously come and go, but once we reach that point in time we officially call "menopause," this new stage of life becomes our permanent reality. In fact, it's at this stage that the real battle has only just begun.

Whether you get slapped around by symptoms, or you float like a butterfly right on through, the fight for your health and well-being is never more important. Once you reach menopause your chances increase significantly of developing diseases that will make you pretty miserable, pretty darn fast. Things like heart disease and stroke, osteoporosis, and some cancers suddenly become a much greater threat. Fortunately, there are things we can do to combat this.

My unique flavor of fitness coaching provides several such tools. These include exercise that works and fits into your life, eating well without diets, prioritizing rest and relaxation, and generally having a whole ton more fun. Of these, I usually find that exercise is the most disliked and misunderstood. It's also arguably the most important.

Many women come to me believing the sole reason to exercise is because they want to lose weight. This is far from the whole truth. It's time to redefine exercise through menopause and its role as we age because it offers us so very much more than that.

Move It Or Lose It

It's a pretty simple and inescapable rule. If you're not moving it, you're gonna lose it. We're not talking about those extra pounds you're hoping will magically fall away from your midsection here. What we're talking about losing is muscle. Losing strength. Losing your mobility... *your very ability to move.* And this directly affects how you're going to age and your quality of life.

Starting around age 30, we naturally begin losing roughly 3–5% of our muscle mass each decade, which then speeds up to 5–10% per decade after age 50. Research also shows that you can lose up to 10% of your muscle mass during the mad hormonal swings of perimenopause alone!

As if that wasn't awful enough, muscle loss, joint issues, and bone loss tend to dance along hand in hand. So we grow weaker, stiffer, achier, and at greater risk for falls and brittle, broken bones. Fun times!

Sadly, I watched my mom fall victim to this trap. A life-long, self-proclaimed anti-exerciser, as she got older and her health declined - and I'm talking high blood pressure, heart failure, and cancer here. Three diseases that could have been improved or perhaps prevented entirely with regular exercise - so too did her mobility decline. Incredibly fast. She had always been an amazing cook, and as far back as I remember she loved nothing more than spending hours in the kitchen, experimenting with ingredients and whipping up some new and delicious dish. In many respects, this *was* her physical activity. It was also her joy. But over time she had trouble with the reaching and bending, the lifting, chopping, and stirring. She couldn't stand for long periods in the kitchen to cook anymore. It was heartbreaking. And she wasn't even that old.

I'm pretty sure you'll be with me on this. Not being able to do the things I love or physically struggling to perform regular daily tasks is nowhere close to how I envision my future or how I desire to age.

The solution to this, of course, is exercise. But that stuff that worked when you were in your twenties and thirties? Chances are it just won't work anymore. It can even backfire and make things worse. You may already have been banging your head against a wall for some time now, trying to figure out what the heck you're doing wrong.

A well-rounded and effective exercise program that gains you real physical benefits and lasting results, includes a balance of cardiovascular, strength, and flexibility training with some balance work and adequate recovery time sprinkled in. This is pretty much the case at any age. But once our regulating sex hormones start to get a bit nuts and eventually tank, the whole equation changes. Our bodies are totally different now, and they don't react the same way to our efforts to keep them healthy and in shape.

So what exactly is a hot and flashy girl to do? Here are my top tips to set you on the menopause exercise success fast track.

Meet Your New BFF

Laura was 54 when she first reached out to me for help. Menopause, long hours sitting at a desk and constant traveling for her business had her feeling heavy, stiff, lacking energy, and very unlike herself.

One of Laura's big fears was that, in her past exercise experiences, her legs had always gotten "HUGE." It made her uncomfortable just to talk about it and she absolutely did not want to look or feel like that again. So once we'd talked about her goals and I explained my approach, including her strength training, she very nearly cut me off at the knees. She was afraid the weights would make her bigger, and at that moment she already felt more than big enough.

Here's the truth. As women, the majority of us are simply not built to get all bulked up and muscley. Our genes and hormones won't allow it. And the only way to combat that natural loss of strength that comes with age, and the inevitable downhill slide that goes with it, is to challenge and build your muscles.

That means making strength training your new exercise BFF. Literally, your best friend for life.

Here are just a few of the benefits of regular strength and resistance training:

- easier performance of your daily activities.
- stronger, more shapely muscles so you look and feel better in your clothes.

- increased muscle increases your metabolism, making you burn more calories, which in turn can help with fat loss. Yay!
- increased bone density and a decreased risk of developing osteoporosis.
- stronger ligaments and tendons and less achy joints.
- better balance and coordination.
- decreased risk of injuries and falls.
- skyrocketed self-confidence, happiness, and well-being.
- better sex.

A higher quality of life and being able to enjoy the crap out of it longer? Who doesn't want to sign up for all that?

If you want to slim down, tone up, and stay strong, fit, and feel youthful over the long haul, regular weight-bearing exercise or strength training is absolutely essential.

Fortunately, Laura trusted me, and I taught her how to train her body to look and feel the way she desired. After we'd been working together for a while, she wrote to me one day, "I wanted thin legs, a nice butt, and great abs - and that's exactly what I am getting. I have lost weight and gained body mass in all the right places, but more importantly, I'm more physically fit than ever. In my 50s and I feel like, and my husband says I look like, I'm in my 30s!"

That's the power of strength training for menopause. And especially with her busy schedule, it was also a lot less time-consuming than she ever imagined was possible.

Less Is More

Here's a little secret for you. I don't love spending hours in the gym. I love exercise and working out. I'm a mega-fan of strength training, what it does, and how it makes me feel (in case you haven't noticed already). I'm also busy and I love a lot of other things too. This is why

I keep my workouts to 20 minutes or less.

It happens to be a bonus that shorter bursts of exercise are more beneficial for menopausal women. There's no need to grind it out for hours in the gym or suffer endlessly on that cardio machine you despise. In fact, that's probably making you feel worse.

Long, drawn-out workouts tend to stress out our bodies. A stressed body is an inflamed body, and an inflamed body will keep you feeling foggy, frustrated, and fat.

When it comes to menopause, less of the right types of exercise is more. It's a lot easier to stick with too.

We Don't Bounce Back Like We Used To

In my late teens and early twenties, I used to go out a lot with friends. Every night was a different venue and we'd drink and dance and laugh and party and drag ourselves home just before the crack of dawn. Quick sleep, head off to work or school, and then we'd do it all over again, night after night, after night. Eventually, the lack of rest would catch up with me, but it took a while.

Now? I still love a good party, but one late night out and it takes me *days* to recover. Maybe you've experienced this too? Our bodies just don't bounce back like they used to.

This applies to exercise as much as it applies to partying it up. Our muscles, joints, and ligaments need time to repair and recover. In fact, it's during recovery that the actual strength-building happens, and *that* is of course our goal.

Working out day after day, after day, especially if you're repeating the same activities and movements over and over again, will very quickly wear you out, increase inflammation, and achieve the opposite of what you're hoping for. Our bodies don't recover like they used to. Allow yours a day or two between those strength workouts to recharge and repair.

Yes. A personal trainer just told you to rest and recover more after exercise. How awesome is that! The time off is not something to fear. I promise, you'll come back even stronger.

Consistency Is Key

You can't do one workout and expect toned thighs and flat abs. You can't eat one salad and expect to drop 20 pounds. One meditation will not transport you into a stress-free zen. I know you already know this.

The key to achieving, and keeping the body and life you want, is in creating consistent and well-balanced fitness habits. Habits that strengthen, nourish, and energize you. Habits that are sustainable now and well into the future. Ones you enjoy and can actually stick with, not because you have to force yourself to, but because they make you feel so incredibly good.

There'll be times when you slip and fall out of the ring. Even your favorite healthy habits will take a tumble now and again. It's called being human. Enough with the guilt and beating yourself up, please. Just jump back in the ring and swing back into action.

Consistency is key. Perfection is absolutely, positively, not required.

Which Will You Choose?

When I was a little girl I used to look at older women and think that the idea of aging gracefully was the most wonderful thing. Now that I've actually reached this age, that's no longer what I aspire to. My mission now is to age awesomely.

To me, aging awesomely means travel, camping, and long walks outdoors. It means still being able to climb on the back of the motorcycle for adventurous rides with my love. It means sharing great meals without worry or guilt. It means once in a while we still tear up the dance floor and party 'til dawn. It means doing it all without preventable physical limits holding me back.

Menopause is no longer the beginning of the end. Rather, it's the beginning of all that's still to come. So…

What does aging awesomely look like to you?

I'll leave you here to give that some thought, along with the final rule of Fight Club:

"If this is your first time at Fight Club, you have to fight."

In this life, there's only one time you'll go through menopause and everything it brings. Aging is inevitable. Aging awesomely is up to you to decide to do.

Fitness - especially exercise - is your secret weapon in the battle to help make that vibrant vision of future-you come true. It's never too late to start, or start again, as many times as necessary. In our menopause version of fight club, you actually do get to choose.

I hope you choose to fight.

To help you get started I've created a free gift exclusively for readers of *Redefining Menopause*. Be sure to grab yours here: https://nicolecabrias.com/redefining-menopause-gift

Brita Doubroff

CEO of Coffer31 Enterprises Inc

https://www.linkedin.com/in/britadoubroff/
https://bit.ly/Me-No-Pause
https://www.instagram.com/stronhger_me.no.pause/
https://britadoubroff.com

Brita Doubroff is a vibrant storyteller who believes in the power of connection and community. With a passion for empowering women, she leads the "me.No.pause!" Facebook group, creating a safe space for women to thrive.

Encouraging women to embrace change with grace and curiosity, Brita believes that our perception and acceptance of menopause transforms our bodies, and evolves our attitudes, beliefs, dreams, and aspirations, which in turn affect our relationships. Drawing from her spiritual journey, filled with wisdom and delight, Brita communicates hope and joy to others.

Refreshingly candid, Brita easily speaks about what she has experienced, what she knows, what she's learning and putting into practice. She's not embarrassed to be frank and ask questions to get the answers she seeks. You can let down your hair and be yourself around her!

Brita believes that by candidly and boldly redefining menopause, that empowerment will help women shape the legacy they will leave for generations to come.

My Doctor Got It Wrong:
How I Survived Menopause

By Brita Doubroff

I was 39 when my doctor delivered the shocking news: "You're in full-blown menopause." In that moment, everything I thought I knew about this phase of life was turned upside down.

Unlike the typical rollercoaster of perimenopause symptoms many women experience, my journey was uniquely different. No hot flashes, no night sweats, no mood swings. Instead, I was experiencing bizarre "electrical surges" that made me feel like I had been plugged into a socket.

My story began with a routine doctor's visit. I hadn't had a period in over a year, but given my history of light, easy cycles, I wasn't particularly concerned. When I mentioned it to my doctor, almost as an afterthought, he suggested a blood test.

The results were shocking. "You're in full-blown menopause," he said. I was stunned. How could I be in menopause without experiencing any of the typical symptoms I'd heard about?

I questioned my doctor, but few resources were available. Back then, menopause was not something people talked about openly. There was no discussion in the media, no TV programs or movies addressing it, and social media didn't exist yet. Occasionally, you'd hear an older woman mention 'her time of life', but never 'menopause' - as if it was a private, taboo word, something to be ashamed of.

The most bewildering part of my experience wasn't just the diagnosis, but the strange "electrical surges" I'd been experiencing since my early 30s. These surges came only at night, transforming my body into a living, buzzing conduit of energy.

Imagine lying in bed, the world quiet around you, when suddenly your entire body feels as if it is stretched taut, fingers and toes extended and rigid, but in reality it isn't. These surges weren't painful, exactly, but deeply unsettling, coming in waves. Sometimes every 20 minutes, lasting for 5 or 10 seconds before ebbing away, only to return with renewed intensity. On particularly bad nights, I'd lie awake feeling 'fried' as if I'd been caught in some bizarre electrical experiment.

I felt isolated and a bit crazy. How could something so strange be happening to my body, and yet no one seemed to know what I was talking about? I started timing these surges, thinking if I had data, I might be believed. Sometimes they would disappear for months, lulling me into a false sense of normalcy, only to return without warning, leaving me feeling vulnerable and confused.

The lack of uncommon menopause symptoms added another layer of complexity to my experience. While my friends complained of hot flashes that left them drenched in sweat or mood swings that made them feel like emotional yo-yos, I was silently battling my own electrical storm. It was a lonely journey, filled with doubt and uncertainty. Was I going through menopause, or was something else entirely wrong with me?

The Search for Answers

Determined to understand what was happening to me, I headed to one of the big bookstores looking for the women's section. To my surprise, there was only one shelf dedicated to Women's health. One shelf. With just ONE book that had 'menopause' in the title. It was as if this major life event that affects every woman was barely worth mentioning. It was disheartening to say the least.

Standing in the aisle, I opened that one book, carefully turning the pages. While raising young kids, we didn't have the funds to buy it. I had felt so alone with nobody to talk to, so I was hoping to find something—anything—that would resonate with my experience.

And then, I saw it. In black and white. A passage describing "electrical surges," a sensation that felt like being plugged into an electrical socket. I couldn't believe my eyes. Here, finally, was someone who knew what I was talking about. I wasn't crazy. I wasn't alone! I stood there in that Bookstore, put my forehead down on the shelf, and I wept, finally feeling seen and validated.

Armed with that tiny bit of new knowledge, I began my climb out of the confusion and isolation that had defined my early experience with perimenopause. Over the years, I have become a health detective, piecing together clues from many various sources like podcasts, books, current research articles and studies to solve the mystery of my own body, but back then, for the most part, the menopause world was still silent for the next 5-7 years. My doctor never asked me about it, and it was still seen as a much older woman's journey. I started experimenting with different ways to manage my symptoms and improve my overall health.

One of the first things I did was to start running. I'd always been active, but now I made it a priority. Multiple bone-density scans showed that being taken off HRT was a mistake that had cost me—without the hormones, my bones had started to deteriorate and I'd been diagnosed with osteopenia, the precursor to osteoporosis. Even this didn't alert my Dr. to the fact something was wrong, that my body needed something.

Running became my way of staying strong, both physically and mentally. It helped me build my bone density, which was crucial, especially after my doctor's early mistake of taking me off HRT (hormone replacement therapy). Along with a regimen of calcium, magnesium, and other supplements, running helped me regain some of that lost bone density. It was hard work, but it was worth it.

When I went to my same doctor at age 51, I went with questions. I'd started to hear about different hormone therapies or progesterone being used. Some friends were using the new bioidentical hormones, and felt better. Maybe I could go on HRT again. I was equipped with questions! Menopause was starting to be talked about a lot more than it had been, and people my age had started talking about it as well, so I didn't feel so alone. Society was obviously still feeling weird using 'the word' and not 'my time of life!' Menopause sounded crass for some reason. Like we feel better about saying 'period' instead of menstruation.

I was shocked to learn that taking me off HRT at 39 had been due to a faulty study, but he remarked it was good that I'd been on it for the last 11 years. When I told him he'd never put me back on it, his admittance, "That was a mistake!" grieved and shocked me. Those simple words carried the weight of 11 years - years that my body could have benefited from HRT's protective effects on my bones, skin, organs, muscles, and brain cells. However, the tragedy didn't end there. After again being misinformed that at 51 years old I was now 'too old' for HRT, it wasn't discussed again.

This whole experience of navigating menopause with incorrect information was like trying to sail through fog with an outdated map. It taught me to chart my own course, to advocate for myself using multiple sources to guide me safely to my destination.

It was a harsh lesson in the consequences of medical oversights and the need for patients to be active participants in their healthcare decisions.

As I opened up about my experiences, I realized that keeping menopause hidden had only made it harder to deal with, so I started talking to friends, family, and anyone who would listen. I wanted to break the silence and make it okay for women to discuss what they were going through.

Today, I'm stronger, healthier, and more vibrant than ever. Despite the challenges I've faced— the misdiagnoses, the mistakes, and the sense of isolation—I've come out on the other side with a renewed sense of purpose and a commitment to living life to the fullest. I've started a Facebook group "me.NO.pause! for women who desire to thrive - not just survive. We discuss the science to break the silence of the female life cycle. It's a supportive community where women can share stories, experiences, tips, travels, hobbies…life! Through this we empower each other. It's a safe place for, "I didn't know that!" where we can laugh and cry about the challenges we face as women, and ultimately celebrate our resilience.

Valuable Lessons Learned

1. Know your family history: Understanding menopause patterns in your family can help you prepare for your own experience. I later discovered that my mom went into menopause at about 43, which explained my early onset.

2. Stay informed and advocate for yourself: Educate yourself through *reliable* sources and don't hesitate to ask questions.

3. Seek support and share your experience: Join supportive communities and share your story. Breaking the silence around menopause can help others feel less alone.

4. Maintain a healthy lifestyle: This phrase is excessively used, but it's TRUTH. Focus on getting enough protein (aim for 120g daily - or 1 gr per lb of weight) and engage in regular weight-bearing exercises. Running and weight training became my way of staying strong, both physically and mentally.

5. Stay physically active: Engage in weight-bearing activities you *enjoy.* Whether it's running, dancing, hiking, or pickleball,

regular exercise boosts overall well-being. A rebounder is excellent for those concerned about their bone density.

6. Monitor your health *regularly*: Keep track of your symptoms and have regular check-ups. After being diagnosed with osteopenia, I became more vigilant about my bone health. Ask for treatments, they won't be offered.

7. Consider Hormone Replacement Therapy: Discuss the option of Bioidentical Hormones with a trusted doctor or Naturopath who is up to date on the latest research around menopause, even during perimenopause to prepare for what's ahead. HRT can help alleviate symptoms, support bone health, increase libido, and more.

8. Embrace a positive outlook: *You* are the creator of your thoughts. And you *can CHOOSE* better thoughts! View menopause as a natural part of life rather than a decline in health or femininity.

9. Practice stress management: Incorporate relaxation techniques into your daily routine to help manage stress and reduce symptoms. Just Do It!

10. Don't take offense: At 34, I made a *conscious choice* never to be offended again. This deliberate choice has made my life easier, richer, and calmer.

Menopause isn't a life sentence or the end of your vibrant years. It can be the beginning of a new, fulfilling phase of life. Despite the challenges I've faced - misdiagnoses, mistakes, and feelings of isolation - I emerged with a renewed sense of purpose and a commitment to living life to the fullest.

My experience underscores the importance of understanding your unique journey, advocating for yourself, and finding credible information and resources to support you along the way. Remember, every woman's menopause journey is unique. There's no one-size-fits-all experience.

The electrical surges that once left me feeling alone and confused have become a reminder of my body's resilience and capacity for change. They've taught me to listen to my body, to seek answers when things don't feel right, and to trust my instincts.

Today, I'm not just surviving menopause; I'm thriving through it!

I've taken the initiative to start a Brand of supplements for women called "Strongher", specifically designed to support women from the beginning of their transition and beyond. It's my way of ensuring that other women have the resources and support I wished for during my journey.

Menopause is not the end of vibrancy; it's the beginning of a new chapter in life, one where understanding and advocating for your health is more crucial than ever. The possibility to live a thriving, active, and joyful life is still very much within reach, and I'm living proof of that.

So, to all the women out there navigating their own menopause journeys, whether you're experiencing common symptoms or unique challenges like my electrical surges: You're not alone. Your experiences are valid, and there's a whole community of women ready to support you. Embrace this new chapter with confidence, armed with knowledge and a positive outlook. Navigating menopause with misinformation was like trying to sail through fog with an outdated map. I learned that sometimes you need to chart your own course, using multiple sources to guide you safely to your destination."

Remember, menopause is a natural transition, not a disease. It's a time to reassess, reinvent, and rediscover yourself. It's an opportunity to prioritize your health, pursue new passions, and deepen your relationships. Yes, there will be challenges, but there will also be triumphs and moments of profound self-discovery.

As you navigate this journey, be patient with yourself. Listen to your body, advocate for your health, and don't be afraid to seek support when you need it. Celebrate your strength, your resilience, and the wisdom you've gained and will continue to gain over the years.

And most importantly, never let anyone tell you that your best years are behind you. *The best is yet to come!* Embrace your menopause journey with open arms, knowing that it's not an ending, but a powerful new beginning. You have the power to redefine what menopause means for you, to challenge societal perceptions, and to thrive in ways you never imagined.

So here's to you, to your journey, and to the vibrant, empowered woman you are becoming. The world needs your wisdom, your strength, and your unique perspective. Embrace it, electrical surges and all, because this is your time to shine brighter than ever before!

Julie Ashlock

Founder and CEO of Jules Body Shoppe

https://www.linkedin.com/in/julieashlock/
https://www.facebook.com/jbodyshoppe
https://instagram.com/julesbodyshoppe
https://julesbodyshoppe.com/
https://julesbodyshoppe.idlife.com/

Julie Ashlock aka "Jules" is a Certified Master Health Coach, Certified Menopause Coaching Specialist, Certified Nutritionist, and Certified Personal Trainer with over 16 years of experience in the health and wellness industry. Passionate about empowering high-achieving women to navigate menopause naturally, Julie has previously brought her expertise and personal journey to the forefront in her first e-book, The Menopause Manifesto: Empowering Women to Thrive. Her unique approach integrates DNA testing, detoxing and customized nutrition, helping women to thrive through this crucial life phase. Julie's personal discovery of her MTHFR (methylenetetrahydrofolate reductase) gene variants has been transformative, enabling her to manage her own menopause journey with excellence and uninterrupted vitality. She is dedicated to guiding others on a similar path to optimal health and well-being during menopause and beyond.

Unlocking The Secrets of Menopause: Genetic Tips Every Woman Should Know

By Julie Ashlock

Menopause can feel like uncharted territory, especially when traditional advice doesn't seem to resonate. But what if the answers lie within your genes? This chapter reveals the critical genetic insights every woman should know to manage menopause with confidence and clarity.

What is MTHFR, and why should it matter to you? The MTHFR gene provides instructions for making an enzyme called methylenetetra hydrofolate reductase. This enzyme plays a crucial role in processing amino acids, the building blocks of proteins.

Statistically, 40–60% of women are affected by having at least one of the MTHFR variants. You may have one or all these variants, which can play a crucial role in how you address your overall health. While there are multiple symptoms associated with each of these variants, the following are a sample of what an individual may experience:

Common MTHFR Variants:

- C677T Variant:

  - Associated with reduced enzyme activity.
  - Can lead to elevated homocysteine levels, affecting cardiovascular health.

- A1298C Variant:

  - Less impact on enzyme activity than C677T.
  - May still contribute to health issues when combined with other genetic or environmental factors.

- Compound Heterozygous (both C677T and A1298C):
  - Greater reduction in enzyme activity.
  - Increased risk for health complications, including during menopause.

When the MTHFR gene variant is present during menopause, various physiological changes can occur due to its influence on methylation processes. Some potential effects of the MTHFR gene variant are:

- Hormonal Imbalance:
  - The MTHFR gene can affect the metabolism of hormones, exacerbating symptoms like hot flashes, mood swings, and sleep disturbances.

- Increased Homocysteine Levels:
  - Women with MTHFR variants may have higher levels of homocysteine, which can increase the risk of cardiovascular issues. Elevated homocysteine is a known risk factor for cardiovascular diseases, which in turn can contribute to cognitive decline and dementia.

- Nutrient Deficiencies:
  - The MTHFR gene can impair the body's ability to convert certain nutrients, leading to deficiencies in folate, vitamin B12, and others, which are crucial during menopause.

- Detoxification Issues:
  - Detox pathways can be less efficient, potentially leading to a buildup of toxins that could worsen menopausal symptoms.

- Mental Health Concerns:

  - The MTHFR gene can impact neurotransmitter production, contributing to anxiety and depression, which can be more pronounced during menopause.

- Bone Health:

  - Impaired methylation may affect calcium metabolism, leading to concerns about bone density and the risk of osteoporosis.

While there are technically 34 recognized symptoms of menopause, I am addressing the most common ones here. General symptoms of menopause are hot flashes, night sweats, brain fog, weight gain, mood swings, and fatigue. Symptoms are exacerbated by the MTHFR variants with higher levels of fatigue, increased risk of depression and anxiety, greater hormone imbalances leading to more severe menopausal symptoms, and higher susceptibility to cardiovascular issues due to elevated homocysteine.

I feel it is crucial to address "brain fog" a little more here. While I am not prone to being an "alarmist," statistics don't lie. Symptoms of brain fog are not uncommon during menopause and may be minor and temporary. However, because women typically live longer than men, the likelihood of developing age-related conditions like dementia increases. Menopause is marked by a significant decline in estrogen production, which can have a direct impact on brain health. This hormonal change can disrupt neural homeostasis, leading to alterations in brain function and an increased risk of cognitive decline.

Estrogen helps maintain vascular health by promoting vasodilation and reducing plaque buildup in arteries. Its decline can lead to an increased risk of cerebrovascular disease, which is closely linked to dementia. Estrogen is also believed to help in the clearance of beta-amyloid plaques, a hallmark of Alzheimer's disease. Lower estrogen levels may contribute to the accumulation of these plaques. The cholinergic system, which is essential for memory and learning, is influenced by estrogen. Reduced estrogen can impair cholinergic function, leading to cognitive decline. Women with certain genetic predispositions, such as those carrying MTHFR variants, may experience compounded risks. The estrogen decline during menopause can intensify the effects of these genetic factors, increasing the likelihood of developing dementia development. Estrogen influences glucose metabolism and insulin sensitivity. Post-menopausal women are at a higher risk of developing insulin resistance, which is also associated with increased dementia risk.

Studies have shown that women who experience early menopause tend to have a higher risk of dementia compared to those who experience menopause later in life. These higher risk studies suggest that the duration of natural estrogen exposure may play a role in cognitive health. I wish I had known this crucial data years ago - I lost my mom last year to dementia and cardiac arrest. She had a hysterectomy when she was 40 years old. I'm sure that she could have had a much different outcome had this vital knowledge been shared with her hysterectomy care.

The decline in estrogen levels during menopause can significantly impact a woman's cognitive health and increase the risk of developing dementia. By understanding these mechanisms, women can seek personalized strategies to maintain estrogen balance and support brain health during this critical period.

Now that we've discussed why you should be aware of whether you actually have one or all of these variants, what steps can you take to identify if you have one, two, or all of them? As a Certified Master Health Coach, Certified Menopause Coaching Specialist, Certified Personal Trainer, and Certified Nutritionist, I have spent the last 16 years studying and experimenting with ways to customize solutions for my clients. What I discovered (and what you may already know) is one size does NOT fit all. You are uniquely you, and your DNA is uniquely yours. Because your DNA contains vital information about you, I present to you a DNA test that is like having your own personal owner's manual. You no doubt have one for your car - why wouldn't you have one for your own body!

What can you expect to find out from your DNA test? In addition to knowing if you have one or more of the MTHFR variants, your results will help you better understand how your body might respond to certain diet choices which may help take your fitness regimen to the next level. Your report includes detailed and unique recommendations that will help you eat better, train better, and live better. Some of the topics covered in your report include aerobic potential, muscle performance, weight regain after dieting, dopamine and food reward, and caffeine metabolism. Remember that this isn't a "one-size-fits-all" approach to nutrition and fitness. Your DNA report is your personalized owner's manual on how your body responds to diet and exercise based on your unique gene profile.

Identifying these specific traits of your DNA can be life-changing on so many levels! I personally have saved so much time, money, and frustration on how I approach my daily habits - what I eat, how I work out, how I supplement, and how I talk to myself (positive self-talk matters!!). I no longer waste time doing too much cardio - my workouts are precise and tailored exactly to what my DNA tells me I need. While I do enjoy spending time in the gym, I realize that many people don't - you simply want to get in, maximize your efforts in the gym, and get out. You are busy, and you need to get on with your 25,000 other priorities!

Most importantly though, I now know how to address the MTHFR gene variants that I personally have. Incorporating my DNA knowledge has given me all the ammunition that I need to thrive through menopause.

Knowing and implementing your DNA traits and strategies is only the first part of how I help my clientele optimize their health. I am a firm believer in the importance of detoxification. We all have a huge buildup of toxins and chemicals that requires our need to detoxify our systems on a regular basis. Why is it important to detox our body, especially during menopause?

Menopause is characterized by fluctuating hormone levels, particularly estrogen and progesterone. The liver plays a critical role in metabolizing and eliminating these hormones. Efficient detoxification helps to maintain hormonal balance and reduce symptoms such as hot flashes, mood swings, and weight gain. As women age, the body's metabolic rate can slow down. Proper detoxification supports the liver's function in metabolizing fats, proteins, and carbohydrates, while also promoting a healthy weight and energy levels.

Over the years, environmental toxins, medications, and processed foods can accumulate in the body. Detoxifying the liver, kidneys, and intestines helps in eliminating these toxins, reducing the burden on these organs, and improving overall health. A healthy digestive system, with cleansed intestines, enhances the absorption of essential nutrients that are crucial for managing menopausal symptoms and maintaining overall health. Chronic inflammation is common during menopause and can exacerbate symptoms. Detoxification helps lower inflammation by removing irritants and toxins that contribute to inflammatory processes. Additionally, toxin build-up can affect mental clarity and mood. A detoxified system supports better mental health and cognitive function, which is especially important during the hormonal transitions of menopause. A clean system is more efficient in fighting off infections and illnesses. Detoxifying helps support a robust immune system, which can be compromised during menopause due to hormonal changes.

While there are many different options on the market, the option that I recommend a 3-phase system formulated from all-natural ingredients.

Phase 1: Kidneys and Bowels

Your kidneys and bowel make up your body's secondary filtration system. Beginning the detox process here helps create a foundation for maximizing your results.

Phase 2: Detoxification

The body's primary all-purpose filtration system is the liver, which filters everything you consume before dumping waste into either the kidneys or bowel. During this phase you experience a new "normal" to your daily routine as your body begins to work efficiently and how it was designed.

Phase 3: Restoration

The gut is the "brain" of your immune system. We've all heard that our gut is our second brain, right? In this phase the focus is on supplying the nutrients your body craves to support restoring the gut to a state of homeostasis.

My first 30-day detox was pretty mind-blowing. By addressing chronic inflammation (which I confirmed was an issue for me via my DNA results), I lost a total of twelve inches around my mid-section and arms! The really incredible (and surprising) part of my detox experience was that I only lost a total of three pounds! Chronic inflammation is so prominent for so many women, and knowing how to effectively address it makes all the difference in the world. The second outcome I was absolutely not expecting was that I no longer was experiencing night sweats! None! They were gone!

It is really amazing that when we give our body the things that it is desperately seeking, we find changes that we have needed for so long.

Now that we have discovered how to unzip our genes and rid ourselves of unwanted toxins and inflammation. What's next?

The third portion of the equation is to fill in our nutritional gaps. In today's generation, as much as we seek to provide nourishment to our body via whole foods (lean proteins, complex carbohydrates, and healthy fat), it is virtually impossible to provide our body with all that it needs nutritionally. What we were able to get through food in the 1970s is now non-existent due to GMOs (genetically modified organisms), antibiotics injected into our protein sources, chemicals sprayed on the crops, and processed "foods."

The solution that I discovered is to customize my nutritional supplements. The concept that one size does not fit all, absolutely applies here. How does it even make sense that you and I would possibly need the same nutritional supplements? Our DNA is completely different.

Note: there is a HIPAA-compliant health assessment (meaning that no one will ever see your personal information) for both the nutritional supplements and DNA test results.

The supplements that I offer to my clients are pharmaceutical-grade, gluten-free, soy-free, non-GMO, and chronobiologically designed for what your body needs during the day while your systems are active versus what it needs at night while your systems are at rest. You are also assured that you will not be recommended any supplements that may be harmful to any potential medications that you are taking.

One of the many benefits of customizing your nutritional supplements is, for those who do have an MTHFR variant, the proper form of methylated folate will be consumed. Why does this matter?

Methylated folate, often referred to as 5-MTHF (5-methyltetra hydrofolate), is the active form of folate that the body can use directly in various metabolic processes. Unlike regular folic acid, methylated folate does not need to undergo additional conversion in the body.

Individuals with MTHFR gene variants have a reduced ability to convert folic acid into its active form. Methylated folate bypasses this inefficient conversion process, ensuring that these individuals can still get the active form of folate they need. Folate is essential for converting homocysteine into methionine. Elevated homocysteine levels can increase the risk of cardiovascular diseases and cognitive decline. Methylated folate helps maintain healthy homocysteine levels, thus reducing these risks. Using methylated folate ensures that individuals with MTHFR variants or other issues absorbing or metabolizing regular folic acid can still meet their body's folate needs effectively. This is vital for overall health, mental well-being, cardiovascular health, and much more.

Having understood the necessity for the highest grade supplementation available, you have the benefit of including methylation+ in your daily routine. Methylation+ is a cutting-edge supplement that harnesses the power of methylated forms of vitamins B9 (folate) and B12, along with trimethylglycine (betaine Anhydrous), to enhance the body's uptake and metabolism of these crucial B vitamins. Moreover, the formula is enriched with a patented form of phosphatidylserine, which facilitates the methylation process by identifying and eliminating dead, damaged, and toxic cells.

This unique blend of vital nutrients is particularly essential for women with MTHFR genetic markers, as it ensures greater bioactivity, maximizes absorption, and optimizes cellular uptake.

I realize that there have been a lot of very scientific explanations throughout this chapter, but I believe it is vitally important to understand that how you identify and address MTHFR and how it relates to your menopause experience matters. My hope in writing this chapter is that you now feel more knowledgeable, heard, understood and empowered to take this information and put it into action. To learn more about these products, and to purchase, if desired, I welcome you to reach out to me at info@julesbodyshoppe.com.

Lisa Feveck

Natural Beauty Ltd
Registered Dietitian & Transformation Coach

https://www.linkedin.com/in/lisa-feveck
https://naturalbeautyltd.com/
https://calendly.com/the_menomorphosis_dietitian/

Lisa Feveck is a dedicated dietitian, educator and transformation coach with a deep passion for women's health issues, in particular, menopause. As a native of the Caribbean island of Trinidad and Tobago, she has a profound understanding of the unique challenges that Caribbean women face during this transformative stage of life. Her approach is compassionate and holistic, focusing on overall health and well-being, and she is especially committed to supporting those who either cannot or choose not to use traditional medications.

Through her personalized coaching programs, Lisa integrates the power of nutrition, fitness and mindset to guide women on their menopausal journey. Her mission is to ensure that every woman feels seen, supported and empowered to advocate for her own health. She believes that menopause is not just a transition but also an opportunity for curiosity and self-discovery, and she is passionate about supporting women to live their best life.

From Perimenopause to Purpose: Redefining Menopause in the Caribbean

By Lisa Feveck

Menopause is often reduced to clichés about hot flashes and mood swings, but my journey was anything but typical. It started in my 30s, not with these well-known symptoms, but with an unsettling array of issues that left me bewildered. My hair began to thin, my heart raced uncontrollably, and, to my utter confusion, I developed a persistent toothache. Doctors and well-meaning friends dismissed my concerns, thinking it was due to the stress of losing my father to cancer. But deep down, I knew something more profound was happening. My body was sending me signals I couldn't ignore, leading me into a journey that would redefine my understanding of menopause—and ultimately, my life's purpose.

The Struggle to Find Answers

My condition grew worse, with muscle and joint pain, digestive issues, and an overwhelming sense of anxiety and depression. Crying at the simplest things became my new normal. Then came the brain fog and memory loss— imagine walking into a room and not knowing why you were there, or forgetting friends' names, or just feeling like your brain was detached and you couldn't think straight. It felt as if I had been put into a different body—one that didn't feel like mine anymore.

The diagnoses I received from doctors never felt right either, especially since my blood tests came back normal. Something was missing, as if a crucial piece of the puzzle was out of place. The hardest part though was the isolation. I felt alone, with no one truly understanding what I was going through. My mother's menopausal experience was typical— mostly hot flashes, so she couldn't relate. As a healthcare professional,

I felt like a failure. How could I help others if I couldn't help myself? This "imposter syndrome" gnawed at me, which only deepened my anxiety and made me question my capabilities.

The Unique Challenges of Menopause in the Caribbean

Menopause in the Caribbean comes with its own set of challenges that are deeply intertwined with our culture, climate, and healthcare system. The sweltering heat intensifies hot flashes; making relief nearly impossible when simply stepping outside can trigger a wave of discomfort. Menopause also remains a taboo subject in many Caribbean communities, leading to a lack of open dialogue and support. This cultural silence often leaves women feeling isolated, navigating this challenging phase alone, without the understanding or empathy of those around them. Even at work, the topic is often brushed aside, and some women quietly leave their jobs, too exhausted or overwhelmed to continue.

These challenges extend to our healthcare system as well. Many doctors here aren't trained to recognize the full spectrum of menopausal symptoms, so issues like dry mouth or tingling in the hands and feet often go unexplained or misdiagnosed, causing women to feel frustrated and misunderstood.

The lack of Caribbean–focused research on menopause only adds to this frustration, making it hard for women to receive care that considers our unique experiences. Treatment options can be limited or inappropriate, leaving many women without effective solutions. These factors combine to create an environment where menopause is not only physically challenging but also emotionally taxing, with women often feeling disconnected from their own bodies and unsupported by the very systems meant to care for them.

Discovering My Purpose

The turning point for me came when I realized I just couldn't take another prescription for yet another symptom. This wasn't the life I wanted for myself. Living in Trinidad and Tobago, it was hard to find answers that made sense for my unique experience. So I went back into research, determined to understand what was happening to my body. That's when I discovered I was in perimenopause. Finally, a diagnosis that made sense! The brain fog lifted, both literally and figuratively, as I began my journey to healing. I had been a dietitian for several years at this point; dedicating my time and energy to helping others achieve better health. But now, I had to help myself first.

The process of healing myself helped me discover my true purpose. One morning, as I reflected on my journey, it hit me—I wasn't just meant to help people with their general health anymore. My own struggles had unlocked a deeper calling. My goal was to help women, especially those in the Caribbean, in understanding and navigating menopause with a sense of empowerment, not confusion.

I saw first-hand how challenging it was to navigate this phase of life without the right support or resources. This lack of conversation and cultural understanding motivated me to create a space where women could feel heard, understood, and supported. I knew I had to take what I learned from my own experience and turn it into something meaningful. It wasn't just about treating symptoms anymore; but helping women transform their lives.

Developing Holistic Approaches

This journey helped me create holistic approaches that address the unique needs of Caribbean women. Through research, I was shocked to learn there were over a hundred possible symptoms of menopause. Suddenly, it all made sense—why menopause was so difficult to diagnose and why so many women suffer without knowing what's happening.

Some symptoms, like dry eyes or dizziness, are subtle and can be easily overlooked. Others, like brain fog or intense anxiety, may be more obvious but are often misunderstood by healthcare providers. Imagine dealing with weight gain, a burning tongue, or even heart palpitations, and not knowing that these could all be linked to menopause. Then there are the emotional and cognitive changes, such as intense anxiety, overwhelming sadness, or the infamous brain fog that can make it difficult to remember simple tasks or find the right words in a conversation. Blurry vision, decreased libido, and even ADHD—all of these can be part of the menopausal experience, yet they often go unrecognized by healthcare providers.

Understanding that menopause is not a one-size-fits-all experience has been pivotal, and my practice has evolved to reflect this. Every woman's journey is unique, so I create solutions that address the whole person—not just the symptoms. We start with a comprehensive checklist to uncover the specific symptoms affecting my clients' quality of life. Often, they believe their symptoms are isolated and unrelated to menopause, so it's always rewarding to witness their "lightbulb moment" when they see they're all interconnected. From there, we embark on a holistic journey together, integrating healthy foods, regular physical activity, and most importantly, fostering a positive mindset to manage their symptoms.

Take Rochelle, for instance. For years, she struggled with uncontrolled blood sugars, fatigue, and brain fog. Only through our sessions did we uncover perimenopause as the root cause, a diagnosis that no one else had considered. By making strategic dietary adjustments, incorporating a regular exercise routine that was right for her body, and practicing mindfulness techniques, Rochelle found relief. More importantly, she regained her sense of self—she felt "normal" again!

Solutions for Caribbean Women

In my work with clients, I've developed a range of strategies specifically tailored to address the unique challenges of menopause in the Caribbean. These approaches have proven effective in helping women navigate this phase of life with greater ease and even joy. I wanted to share some of these strategies with you:

1. **Emphasizing Plant-Based Foods:**

   - A diet rich in plant-based foods can provide all the nutrients you need. Remember, **all plant foods are superfoods,** and it's important to eat foods from the five colour groups daily. Local fruits and vegetables like mangoes, West Indian cherries, cauliflower, melongene (eggplant), and callaloo are packed with vitamins, minerals, and antioxidants that support overall health and help alleviate menopausal symptoms.

   - You don't have to spend money on imported foods to manage menopause symptoms effectively. Incorporating foods native to your country like dasheen, sweet potatoes, and breadfruit into your diet can help stabilize blood sugar levels, reduce inflammation, and improve energy levels. These foods are not only nutritious, but also readily available and affordable.

   - Focusing on whole, unprocessed foods can help manage weight gain and lower the risk of chronic conditions, especially heart disease.

2. **Engaging in Physical Activity:**

   - Regular physical activity is essential for managing weight, reducing stress, and improving mood during menopause.

The Caribbean offers a natural playground for staying active, from walking on the beach to hiking in the hills.

- Taking advantage of the beautiful outdoor environment can make exercise more enjoyable and accessible. Activities like swimming in the sea, walking along scenic trails, or practicing yoga on the beach not only keep the body fit but also nourish the soul.

- You don't have to pay for an expensive gym membership to get exercise. Any physical activity can bring health benefits, once you do it consistently. Engaging in activities like dancing or gardening can be just as effective as a workout. I encourage all my clients to dance to Caribbean rhythms of soca, calypso, or reggae as a fun and engaging way to stay active. The key is finding joy in moving your body regularly.

3. **Practicing Mindfulness and Relaxation:**

- Managing stress is key to navigating menopause with grace and resilience. The Caribbean's serene landscapes offer the perfect backdrop for practicing mindfulness and relaxation techniques. Meditating by the river banks, with the soothing sound of water flowing and the gentle breezes blowing, can help calm the mind and reduce anxiety.

- Spending time in nature, especially when you go barefooted, can reduce stress and improve mental clarity. This practice, known as "grounding," allows for a deep connection with the natural world and promotes overall well-being.

- Incorporating local herbal teas into your diet like lemongrass, ginger, or hibiscus can offer both relaxation and health benefits. These teas can soothe the digestive system, improve sleep, and provide a moment of calm in a busy day.

4. **Building a Support Network:**

- Having a strong support network is essential during menopause. In the Caribbean, community and family are integral parts of life, and these connections can be leveraged to create a supportive environment.

- Joining or forming a support group where women can share their experiences and tips can be incredibly empowering. These groups provide a safe space to discuss challenges and celebrate successes.

- Raising awareness about menopause among family and friends can help create a more understanding and supportive environment. Educating those around us about what menopause entails can reduce stigma and foster empathy.

How I Redefined Menopause

Connecting personal transformations with a broader purpose has been one of the most rewarding aspects of my work. Menopause, a stage of life that's often shrouded in fear and misinformation, has taught me invaluable lessons. One of the most profound is that as long as we're alive and on "this side of the grass," we get to be curious and explore opportunities for growth. Menopause is something that every woman will experience—denying it won't make it go away. How we navigate this journey, however, is largely within our control. We have the power to make choices that shape our experience, turning what is often seen as a daunting phase into one of empowerment and joy.

These challenges have also fuelled my passion and commitment to redefine menopause for women, not only in Trinidad and Tobago and in the Caribbean, but worldwide. This is not just a job for me—it's a calling. My personal journey through menopause, combined with the experiences of the women I work with, has shown me that we can approach this phase of life with strength, balance, and joy. We don't have to conform to the outdated narratives that portray menopause as the end of our vitality or femininity. Instead, we can see it as a time to reclaim our health, our purpose, and our sense of self.

This is how I've redefined menopause, and why my mantra has become, "You can't always change their outcome, but you can change their experience." My name is Lisa Feveck, and I'm a menopause dietitian and coach who uses holistic approaches to support women on their menopausal journey, especially if you cannot or choose not to use traditional medications. For those of you who are ready to redefine menopause for yourselves, click **here** to book a FREE Menopause Makeover session with me!

Meg Johnson Hall

First Quality Consulting
Founder, Senior Healthcare Consultant & Leadership Coach

https://www.linkedin.com/in/meg-johnson-ms-rn/
https://firstqualityconsulting.com/

Hello, I'm Meg Johnson Hall MS, RN, NEA-BC, Founder of First Quality Consulting, your partner for creating effective healthcare practices and operations, and your catalyst for career, life and leadership transitions. I have a bachelor's degree in nursing, a master's degree in healthcare administration and numerous certifications in nursing, leadership, coaching, NLP, and public speaking.

My 40 years of experience in the healthcare industry range from nursing, operations administration, program development and ambulatory care to working as an executive with large multistate healthcare systems. I love to support healthcare practices to re-design for efficiency, safety, quality, and financial viability.

With 20+ years as a leadership coach and mentor to healthcare leaders, 15 years in wellness, I understand the pressure of working in the healthcare sector and how it can make you exhausted, stressed and burned out. I will help you lead and live a more authentic, balanced, and joyful life.

Fighting for Quality of Life

By Meg Johnson Hall

During my mid-40s – I was in a true transition in life. I was recently divorced, my last child had just left the nest, I had moved from Minnesota to Arizona, and started a new job. I thought this was a whole new beginning; how exciting. But then reality hit me, and I realized that I had inherited 500,000 in debt from the divorce, paying alimony, had two properties to take care of, had an aging mother, was learning how to parent two adult children, and was feeling a bit overwhelmed and quite stressed.

In addition, I was experiencing the joy of being in my mid-40s by having almost every possible symptom of menopause. I thought life would get near perfect when I reached this point, but I did not feel it. I needed help in getting through all of this. I went to see a counselor, and she said, with all your menopause symptoms, you need to get that managed as it is interfering with every aspect of your life.

A few days later, I was sitting at my desk in an infusion center that I was the manager of; I had my head in my hands and had tears coming out of my eyes. I loved my job and my staff, but it felt like most of the rest of my life was in a tailspin. One of my charge nurses came into the office, looked at me, and asked, "What in the world is wrong?" She might have been sorry that she had asked that question. Several minutes later I was still listing all of my symptoms and struggles and sharing that I felt I was already in menopause even in my 40s.

After that nice wide opening, I shared what I had been struggling with for at least 5 years. I had been to numerous doctors and felt no better than I did when this all started. I shared the challenges I was facing. So tired all the time that I barely make it through the day and head to bed when I get home; I have hot flashes off and on all day, night sweats at night so bad I have to get up to change the sheets and my PJs, I had gained about 15 pounds, I struggle to focus, concentrate, I was losing the hair that I had finally gotten back after struggling with hypothyroidism for years. I also felt irritable a lot and had to work hard not to let it show, I had no libido, and life had become a real struggle with all these challenges, and I was wondering what my purpose was and if I would ever really enjoy life again.

She chuckled – which was not the reaction I expected. She explained that she had pretty much all those same symptoms and finally found a solution and feels so much better. I told her I had a hard time believing it as I had been to so many doctors, and they just kept telling me to see someone else. I had been to my primary care MD, and it was suggested I go see a menopause specialist. I went to them, and they told me I was suffering from depression and referred me to a psychiatrist. I then went to see the psychiatrist, and they told me that I was going through menopause and to see a menopause specialist or go back to my PCP.

I asked several of these doctors to test my hormone levels, but no one thought it would do any good because they were probably all normal. They also said that since my grandmother had breast cancer in her 80s, hormone therapy would not be an option for me, even if my levels were low. This whole process made me feel even worse than I initially did. I had been through a similar experience when I started having signs of hypothyroidism about 12 years prior. It took over five years to get that issue identified and treated.

I did my research and read many articles. It seemed I had all the classic symptoms.

When I read some of the articles, here is what they stated. As I went down the list – I had almost everyone.

Menopause is natural, but that does not make it easy. My mother had a complete hysterectomy at age 30. I remembered her struggles, and she could not get any help. Some of what I learned about this process our bodies go through I already knew as a nurse, but it is different, like most medical diseases or processes, when you are going through it yourself. Some of the symptoms associated with menopause are outlined below.

Menopause is a natural biological process marking the end of a woman's menstrual cycle, diagnosed after going 12 months without a menstrual period. It usually occurs in women in their late 40s or early 50s but can vary.

Symptoms can vary widely but commonly include:

1. Hot Flashes: Sudden feeling of warmth, often most intense over the face, neck, and chest.
2. Night Sweats: Hot flashes that occur at night and can disrupt sleep.
3. Irregular Periods: Periods may become less frequent before they stop altogether.
4. Vaginal Dryness: Reduced lubrication can cause discomfort and pain during intercourse.
5. Mood Changes: Increased risk of mood swings, irritability, and depression.
6. Sleep Problems: Difficulty falling asleep, staying asleep, or getting restful sleep.
7. Weight Gain: Metabolism slows down, leading to weight gain.
8. Thinning Hair and Dry Skin: Hair can become thin and skin dry and less elastic.
9. Loss of Breast Fullness: Breasts may lose tissue and become less full.

Treatment focuses on relieving symptoms and improving quality of life:

1. Hormone Replacement Therapy (HRT):

- Estrogen Therapy: Effective for relieving menopausal symptoms but associated with risks such as blood clots and certain cancers.
- Progesterone Therapy: Often combined with estrogen to reduce risks.

Note – that the research back then did not mention bioidentical hormones.

2. Non-Hormonal Medications:

- Antidepressants: Low doses can reduce hot flashes and mood swings.
- Gabapentin: Can help reduce hot flashes.
- Clonidine: Used for high blood pressure, may help with hot flashes.

3. Vaginal Estrogen:

- Creams, Tablets, or Rings: Directly applied to relieve vaginal dryness.

4. Lifestyle Changes:

- Diet: Balanced diet with plenty of fruits, vegetables, and whole grains.
- Exercise: Regular physical activity to manage weight and improve mood.
- Stress Reduction: Techniques like yoga, meditation, and deep-breathing exercises.

5. Alternative Therapies:

- Herbal Supplements: Some women find relief with black cohosh, phytoestrogens, and other supplements (consult a healthcare provider).

- Acupuncture: May help reduce symptoms for some women.

6. Bone Health:

- Calcium and Vitamin D Supplements: Important for maintaining bone density.
- Weight-Bearing Exercises: Such as walking or weight training to strengthen bones.

It's essential to consult with a healthcare provider to tailor a treatment plan based on individual symptoms, health history, and risk factors.

I was pretty skeptical when my charge nurse shared her experience. But after thinking about it for a couple of days, I asked her for this doctor's information. I looked at that business card for a few days and then finally decided to give them a call.

The office was wonderful when I called them. I had an appointment within a week. I shared my tale of woes with the doctor, and he shook his head and said I wish I had a dollar for every woman that comes in here with a similar story. He asked dozens of questions, did an exam, drew many labs, and a couple of days later, I got a call to schedule a follow-up visit.

When I went in for that follow-up visit, I partially expected to hear the same old story, but I did have a glimmer of hope since the labs were drawn. As I sat and listened to the findings, I began to cry. Someone had listened to me, completed the assessment, and had an action plan. I had basically no estrogen left in my system; my progesterone was also deficient, as well as my testosterone, and I had issues with my vitamin B and vitamin D levels.

I shared that this was all great to know, but I had been told that I could not have hormone therapy since my grandma got breast cancer in her 80s. He shared that this was not absolute, and there was also an option called bio-identical hormones, which had a much lower risk and had fabulous results in his patients. He shared a few studies that had been done, and I was speechless. I had choices to make on how we did the therapy and was given the option to start a temporary program. Within a week, I already felt a bit better. Within a month, I felt almost back to myself. I was able to concentrate, my hot flashes were very minor – a hand fan would get me through them, I could sleep through the night again, and my mood was improving.

Over the next several years, my life was renewed. I was able to function well at work again, I was able to stay awake in the evening to cook dinner, read, go for a walk, or work on projects. I felt "normal" again. I have continued this therapy for over ten years and have made some adjustments based on labs combined with symptoms with the doctors; luckily, I found others also believed in alternatives. I added better stress management, added meditation, increased my exercise, taking more time to enjoy my interests and hobbies. This leads to more joy in my life. I even found my true love in my 50s.

Here is some basic information that has come out about bioidentical hormones –

Bioidentical hormones are man-made hormones that are chemically identical to those the human body produces. They are often marketed as being more natural or safer than conventional hormone replacement therapy (HRT). These hormones are used to treat symptoms of menopause, perimenopause, and other hormonal imbalances.

Types of Bioidentical Hormones

Bioidentical hormones can include:

- Estrogen (estradiol, estriol)
- Progesterone

- Testosterone
- Dehydroepiandrosterone (DHEA)
- Thyroid hormones

Forms of Bioidentical Hormones

They come in various forms, such as:

- Pills
- Patches
- Creams and Gels
- Injections
- Vaginal Suppositories

Custom-Compounded vs. FDA-Approved

Custom-Compounded Hormones: Pharmacies make these hormones according to a healthcare provider's prescription for an individual patient. The FDA does not regulate them, and they can vary in dosage and purity.

- FDA-Approved Hormones: Standardized and regulated by the FDA for consistency and safety. Examples include estradiol and progesterone products.

I have used both FDA-approved hormones and custom compounded. Both are by top-rated pharmacies.

Benefits

- Symptom Relief: Can effectively relieve menopausal symptoms such as hot flashes, night sweats, mood swings, and vaginal dryness.
- Customized Treatment: Custom-compounded bioidentical hormones can be tailored to an individual's specific hormonal needs.

Risks and Considerations

- Lack of Regulation: Custom-compounded hormones are not FDA-regulated, leading to some practitioner's concerns about consistency, safety, and efficacy.
- Health Risks: Like conventional HRT, they may carry some risks such as blood clots, stroke, and certain cancers, especially if not adequately monitored.

Scientific Evidence: There is some limit to the amount of evidence supporting that bioidentical hormones are safer and more effective than traditional HRT.

Consultation with Healthcare Provider

It's crucial to consult a healthcare provider to determine the best treatment option. They can:

- Assess Symptoms: Evaluate symptoms and health history.
- Monitor Treatment: Regularly monitor hormone levels and adjust dosages.
- Discuss Risks and Benefits: Provide information on bioidentical hormones' potential risks and benefits.

Conclusion

Bioidentical hormones can be a viable option for managing menopausal symptoms, but they should be used under the guidance of an educated healthcare provider to ensure safety and effectiveness.

Once my medical symptoms greatly improved, I was able to succeed more in my career, became interested in doing more fun activities with friends, started dating again, got involved with hobbies and exercise more, and subsequently lost weight. I had hoped that the rest of my life could be productive and fun and maybe include finding a fulfilling partner.

I have grown so much in the last 10–15 years by increasing my self-esteem, extensive self-reflection, personal growth, and finding new outlets I also started education so that I can help people heal naturally through healing touch, nutrition, meditation, and providing life and leadership coaching that is focused on a holistic approach and encouraging everyone to find and life to their authentic self and find their true purpose that not only fills their cup, but the cups of others.

I share this story not to recommend bioidentical hormones but rather instead to ask all of you to be your own advocate; when you know something is wrong, don't give up, but continue to pursue some help, keep knocking on doors until you find someone willing to work with you. Find a health coach to help you explore to be your best self. Whether it is the medical causes of menopause that need either traditional hormones, bioidentical hormones, meditation, essential oils, herbal therapy, or acupuncture, along with better diet, exercise, and stress management. Attacking these issues head-on can help you have a fantastic life during and after menopause. I have learned that having a holistic approach to any of life's challenges will result in better outcomes and improve your quality of life.

I am forever grateful to my charge nurse, who helped open my eyes and opened a door for me to live a truly amazing middle age. I now enjoy helping others to find that amazing middle-age life as well.

Jen Kunkel

Wild Savvy
Midlife Women Wellness & Lifestyle Strategist

https://www.linkedin.com/in/jenkunkel/
https://www.facebook.com/jenkunkel
https://instagram.com/jen_kunkel
https://wildsavvy.com/
https://www.jenkunkel.com/

Hi, my name is Jen Kunkel and I believe the way our society deals with menopause and aging is antiquated.

We've got menopause wrong. It's not a disease to be cured… pushing drugs and HRT.

This might bandaid the symptoms, but it rarely results in improved wellness.

I advocate for embracing midlife with a holistic, high vibration, purposeful lifestyle that empowers YOU… A woman who wishes to take personal responsibility for every aspect of her own well being.

We can choose to NOT put our health and future into the hands of doctors who are clueless about what we're going through.

Let's thrive by creating a quality of life that provides us with autonomy and choice as we age.

My mission is to help women embrace the natural evolution of menopause, like a beautiful butterfly emerging into her next chapter with purpose, passion, joy and adventure.

Enchanted Menopause: An Energetic Shift to Embrace Our Magical Metamorphosis

By Jen Kunkel

The world spun frantically around me as I stood there, in the middle of my kitchen, frozen and unable to move. A whirlwind of jumbled thoughts and images crashed in on me, all at once.

Suddenly dizzy and disoriented, I couldn't catch my breath.

Stop.

What is happening?!

I steadied myself and thought, "Oh my gosh! Am I having a panic attack?"

A few moments ago, I was putting away groceries. Now I'm spinning out with anxiety.

Breathe, Jen.

This had never happened before and only one more time since… a few days later.

I'll tell you how I stopped it, and how I made sure it never happened again.

But first…

In my late 40s, I started feeling emotionally 'off'.

I often had strange thoughts, trouble sleeping and questioned my sanity.

I was clueless this was about menopause, so going to a doctor never entered my mind. I prefer holistic wellness, so I doubt I'd have rushed to get medical attention anyway.

Now I know what was behind the anxiety, wild thoughts, depression, and massive lack of energy I was experiencing. These were all symptoms of perimenopause.

I want you to know that if you're feeling any of these things, it is normal. You're not going crazy.

I turned it around, even before I knew why it was happening.

Thankfully, I've meditated for years and was able to ground myself fairly quickly.

In a way, the panic attacks were a blessing. They inspired me to recommit to the mind-body practices that ultimately got me through it all, with my peace intact.

Now, I experience almost no menopause symptoms and move through life with peace and joy. I no longer feel sidelined from my life and business. I've stopped barely surviving and instead operate with peak physical and emotional wellness.

I Took Control of My Physical and Mental Well-being and You Can Too

It's a myth that menopause has to be hard and painful.

It can be easy. I can show you how to find peace with the same simple mind-body tools I use.

Studies show mindfulness helps with menopause anxiety and other symptoms. My personal experience proved it for me.

Maybe you've tried meditation or mindfulness practices before and thought they didn't work for you or it was too hard.

Most people make it too complicated or don't understand the missing piece.

I make it easy with my unique and customizable menu of mind-body practices, combined with simple lifestyle tweaks to optimize your endocrine system for hormonal balance.

It's not complicated. Anyone can do it, when you do it my way.

Go to the link below for a simple breathing meditation
you can start with.
https://www.jenkunkel.com/squarebreath

Is This My Life Now?

I'll give it to you straight. It hasn't been all rainbows and butterflies since I halted the anxiety and panic of perimenopause.

A few years after the panic attack turmoil and turnaround, I still didn't know it was all part of menopause and my mindfulness practices slipped to the wayside.

I woke up one morning and realized I had gained 15 pounds... overnight.

(Not really overnight, but it sure seemed that way... you might know what I mean.)

I felt bloated, swollen, stiff, and depressed.

I did NOT want to get out of bed.

Every day, I thought, "Well, this is my life now."

It was a horrible conclusion to come to because I've always been relatively fit.

In my 20s, I often worked out twice a day.

Then at 50-something, I didn't recognize myself.

One day I decided…

No! I do NOT accept this is my life now.

And I started taking steps to change it.

I dragged myself out of bed and went for a daily walk, even if it was only a few minutes.

I paid more attention to eating a healthy diet.

I recommitted to meditation and mindfulness practices and delved deeper into emotional release, energetic healing, and shadow work.

That decision changed everything.

Just like another decision I made in my past…

Inspiration to Live Fully: Correcting a Wrong Turn in Life

Growing up, I was super shy and struggled to express myself.

As a young adult, I was the good girl… the responsible, reliable rule follower.

I was on track to check off all the boxes for the conventional idea of a happy, successful life…

Marriage… check!

College… check!

Career… check!

Have 2.4 kids… Whoa!! Not yet!

Let's back up to "marriage"…

From the outside, it looked fine.

In reality, it wasn't.

I was 24 and finally got married after 4 years of dating. He negotiated with me to quit work and go to school full time, to move to Albuquerque, away from my family and near his. It was only supposed to be for a few years.

I got my degree in Chemical Engineering and found a lucrative job at a good company. He wouldn't agree to move back to Vegas, as originally planned.

Though I went to work for a good company, it wasn't the job I envisioned and I had zero passion for it. I wanted to do something that made a more direct impact on people's lives.

My marriage felt empty.

I'd often make dinner for two and end up eating alone.

I felt more lonely when he was home than when he wasn't.

His go-to spot was on the couch, remote in hand, flipping between a basketball game and political news. "Wait for commercial," he'd say if I talked to him. But there never was a commercial, because he'd always flip to another channel.

Counseling didn't work because he was already checked out of the marriage.

Still in my twenties, my life was hollow and I was becoming an empty shell.

It felt like I had taken a wrong turn in life and the path I was on kept sweeping me further away from the life I was meant to live.

After 6 years, and a great deal of self-reflection and prayer, I decided to get out... with no protest from him... He was out a long time ago.

I moved back to Las Vegas!

And I thank God for guiding me to this decision. Even though some might say God would not approve, I feel I had His blessing and guidance and that He did not create me to live that miserable life.

I am blessed by that decision.

It led me to a career path that allows me to help people in the way I always imagined and to experience precious moments with family, I would have otherwise missed.

I stepped off the edge of a cliff, not knowing what I would find and my life moved in ways I never imagined.

I'm no longer the meticulous rule follower. You see, I believe many of the rules and following the conventional path are not designed in our best interests.

The conventional path has us using untested or inadequately tested ingredients… in our food, in our personal care products, and in our household cleaning products. The medical system wants us to take drugs that can have devastating side effects, for every minor ailment.

I've woken up to societal conditioning that keeps us playing small in life and makes us unwell in many ways.

I've always had a dash of rebel in me, and now I fully embrace her.

My way is off the beaten, conventional path and it's not for everyone.

But maybe it's for you.

I encourage you to let your rebellious side out. Or maybe it's simply your authentic self. Empower yourself to make the rest of your life the healthiest, most enjoyable, most purposeful adventure possible!

I saw this quote by Zach Pogrob that captures what I'm saying beautifully.

"You need goals that give you goosebumps. Friends that give you energy. Lovers that give you butterflies. And a mission that makes it impossible to sleep, and irresistible to wake up. It feels like fireworks inside your mind. So, use excitement as a compass. It shows you exactly where to go."

Questions to contemplate:

What is ONE thing you want that you're holding back from because it doesn't follow convention or social norms or what people expect of you?

What would it take for you to say YES to that?

What's one small step you could take today?

How is menopause and your struggle with it getting in the way?

To live your best life, you must feel your best, physically and emotionally.

What the Conventional Path Tells You about Menopause

Western culture conditions us to believe menopause is a hard, painful struggle. That it's a disease that needs to be cured.

Menopause is not a disease to be cured. It's a natural part of life that we can embrace in a way where it becomes an enchanted experience and a beautiful metamorphosis.

Other cultures embrace menopause as a time of transition to greater wisdom. They treasure their elder women as wise sages.

We are conditioned to believe we are becoming obsolete and insignificant as we age. We're not.

We can embrace this phase of life as a transformation, just as the butterfly transforms from a caterpillar.

And, we don't need to feel forced to resort to medications to do it.

Why Natural Methods?

A couple of decades ago, I decided to start a garden. As I researched where to get the best, most natural seeds, I had no idea the can of worms I was opening.

Much of what I found is a bit off topic for this discussion, so I'll summarize.

I learned about questionable policies and tactics of the companies and agencies that are supposed to protect our food supply and other products we use daily.

Especially in the US, ingredients are allowed in our food, personal care products, cleaning products, medications, and more, that are questionable, at best, and cause cancer, at worst.

You've heard the commercials for medications and the laundry list of side effects, often including possible death.

Ironically, I originally wanted to go into pharmaceutical manufacturing with my degree in Chemical Engineering, concentrating in Biomedical Technology. I can safely say, I'm glad I didn't go that route. I'd likely be a dead whistle-blower by now.

I used to be a highly skeptical, science-backed, prove-it-to-me kind of person. But now I have a firm belief in the body's ability to heal itself.

A cut heals. Broken bones heal. Burns heal. Our bodies heal every day.

Science is beginning to come up with hard evidence that we have more power in self-healing than we once realized.

Access my FREE Menopause Balance Mini Course at
https://www.jenkunkel.com/mbmc

We Are Complete Beings / Energy: Body, Mind & Soul (Remember!)

I first started a daily meditation practice when I was in college. I heard 10 minutes of meditation was equivalent to 4 hours of sleep and I wanted more time, without being tired.

When I'd start to get tired while studying in the student lounge, I'd take a break to go into the ladies' room and pick a stall far away from the door to sit for about 10 minutes. Yes, I sat on the toilet. It was the only place to get privacy and make sure I wasn't disturbed. I'd do a simple progressive relaxation meditation. This would give me the boost of energy I needed for another few hours of studying or completing homework.

You can do the same thing to help boost your energy during menopause.

> Here's a version of that meditation for you to use.
> https://www.jenkunkel.com/relax

But it's more than meditation…

Ultimately, we are energy and our energetic vibration reflects our overall well-being.

We can raise our energetic vibration, release the energy of undesirable imprints, and replace it with the energy of what we prefer to experience.

If you're thinking, "That sounds pretty out there, Jen. I think I'll move on to the next chapter," I get it. I used to be skeptical about this woo-woo energy stuff too. In fact, I outright didn't believe it.

Then I experienced it firsthand.

My massage therapist also did Reiki, a type of energy work. I knew nothing about it, but I wasn't interested.

I had a knot next to my shoulder blade that wouldn't go away, no matter what we did.

She kept asking me to let her do Reiki on it. I kept saying, "No, I want a regular massage. I like the touching. That's what I came for."

One day she talked me into doing a session with the first half massage and the second half Reiki. After that, I was convinced. The Reiki part was so much more relaxing than the massage part. I almost didn't believe it. But I had to. I was there. I experienced it. It was real.

I started researching energy work and shifted the way I was doing meditation. I went deeper into myself, focusing on activating my body's healing mechanisms any time something felt off.

For example, I've used it for a miraculous recovery from spinal injuries. I was rear-ended in a car accident that affected my cervical spine and blew out a disk in my lower back. For almost a year, I had to sit down and hold my leg up with my arms to put my pants on, at only thirty-something. Fusion surgery was recommended and I didn't want it. So, I started focusing my meditations on healing my spine.

Within a relatively short time, the pain subsided and I have had zero issues since then. I haven't had another MRI, so I don't know if it's physically healed, but I know how I feel. And, I firmly believe in the body's ability to heal itself… from anything.

I remember seeing yogis on television when I was a kid, who could slow their breathing to the point where they appeared to be dead. With proper focus, we have control over our bodies, even our autonomic nervous system.

We humans go around as if we understand everything, but we don't.

I question EVERYTHING. And I believe ANYTHING is possible. I'm an open-minded skeptic… It seems like an oxymoron, but it's the only way I could ever imagine being. I don't believe anything blindly. But I believe in possibilities, so anything IS possible.

We are conditioned to believe we are weak and powerless… that we need to depend on so-called experts to 'fix' us. In reality, we have that power within ourselves.

The way I interact with my inner self, my energy, and the energy of the world has transformed my life at every phase.

When I got out of my regular habits, I noticed it. My energy was out of sync and my body and emotional well-being would get out of sync too.

My menopause experience transformed from literally feeling crazy to a feeling of total peace, embracing who I am and feeling physically more well than I have in years. It showed me that the mind-body energy practices were the key to embracing life and menopause with peace and wellness.

You can do this too.

JEN'S SUMMARY OF PRACTICAL TIPS

1. Move your body

Even a simple daily walk will help reset your metabolic system and support balanced hormones.

It also helps reduce inflammation, joint pain, soreness and increase energy.

2. Remove toxins

Food

Personal care products

Cleaning products

Environmental factors (as much as possible)

3. Reset your emotional equilibrium.

Identify your common triggers and implement a plan of quick, simple ways to diffuse them in the moment.

These triggers could be emotional or physical. Maybe you feel anxious in certain types of interactions or with certain people. Maybe drinking red wine triggers a hot flash.

Simple methods to diffuse these triggers could include the square breathing meditation I shared earlier or something as simple as counting to 10 with a deep breath.

4. Restore Balance with specific mind-body practices.

This is where the real shifts happen.

Balance Chakras (Energy Centers)

This is the simplest thing we can do

> Go to this link to experience my
> "Chakra Balancing for Menopause" workshop.
> https://www.jenkunkel.com/chakra

Emotional release

There are several methods you can use and I have developed a few proprietary techniques.

I discovered my 'Eye Of The Storm' emotional release method one day when I was emotionally triggered by something that happened with a family member and a friend. I went into victim mode, feeling everyone was against me, so I went into the bathroom crying. I found myself wallowing in my feelings.

I let myself feel what I was feeling, in a way I never had before. I let myself be angry with the people I loved, and with myself. I cried it out as I allowed myself to fully process feelings that were deep within.

Then, suddenly I had a realization, and everything I had been thinking and feeling almost became funny and ridiculous. I felt a huge sense of relief, release, and peace. I instantly knew this was a practice I would use with clients. I did and it has helped them.

Shadow work

This takes us deeper to release debilitating and low vibe emotional patterns.

5. Daily Habits

Focus on creating simple daily habits to maintain your high energetic vibration. I know, from experience, that when we get out of these habits, our energy shifts back to a low vibe and our wellness suffers, so having an easy, doable way to keep those habits up is critical.

> These tips are the basis for my
> Hormonal Harmony Quest program.
> https://www.jenkunkel.com/hhq

We are conditioned to treat menopause as a disease to be cured and that it's a hard, painful struggle signaling the end of our significance as a woman, when it is actually a natural part of life that we can embrace, with peace and peak health, as we transition to a new phase of wisdom where we become more significant and valuable.

CONNECT WITH JEN

I know this approach is not for everyone and I'm not here to convince you this is the right or only way. But if it resonates with you, if you're ready to stop being sidelined by menopause and get back to living with peak physical and emotional wellness, so you can live your best life, connect with me. I'd love to get to know you better and offer my support.

The BEST way to connect is to get on my VIP Insider List to get podcast, video, and workshop updates, plus tips and relatable stories you won't get anywhere else.

https://www.jenkunkel.com/VIP

You can also go to jenkunkel.com for all my social links, other free goodies and to see current programs I offer to support you in creating your own enchanted menopause experience, so you can transform into the beautiful butterfly you are.

Monica Marrone

Eco-Wellness
Health Coach, Author & Speaker

https://www.linkedin.com/in/monicamarrone
https://www.facebook.com/monica.marrone1/
https://www.instagram.com/livingyoungerlonger/
https://www.monicamarrone.com/
https://monicamarrone.now.site/

My mission is to inspire women over 50 to become their healthiest and best selves so they can serve God and others. My motto is to Be More, Make More, and Give More.

My holistic approach to health - Living Younger Longer, is about not letting your age define who you are, what you can do, and who you are becoming. It's a lifestyle dedicated to growing, learning, exploring, and serving others.

At 66, I'm finding life after menopause exciting and rewarding. I'm leaner, faster, and more fit than I was in my 40's. When I'm not in the kitchen exploring healthy recipes, you might find me running a half marathon, facilitating a group at church, or leading a Grand Canyon hike. I'm growing a tribe of like-minded women who desire a vibrant, healthy, fulfilling life as we age.

Does this speak to your heart? Let's talk.

Menopause—Make It the Best Chapter

By Monica Marrone

The first time I heard women explain what it feels like to get a hot flash, I rolled my eyes and thought. Oh, come on, it can't be that bad. What's the big deal? I was at a conference, and one topic was the launch of products to help menopausal women. And shortly after that, as if to catch me in my skepticism, it happened.

I was visiting my brother, and it had been a stressful, busy day. I was hurrying to get out the door. The wave of heat and tingling started at my waist and moved up my body just like the women described it. The sweat beaded on my forehead, and I could feel my cheeks turning crimson.

I'd entered the club of perimenopausal women. The adventure to understand what was happening to my body and how it would impact my health had begun.

The Not So Good News

Perimenopause: The Rollercoaster Ride

Perimenopause, the transition period leading up to menopause, can feel like an unpredictable rollercoaster. One moment, you're laughing with friends; the next, you're in tears over a commercial. These mood swings are real and bewildering, but understanding that they are part of the process helps you cope.

Hot Flashes: The Unwanted Heatwave

Hot flashes are at the top of most women's menopause symptom list. These sudden waves of heat can strike at any time, leaving you drenched in sweat and desperate for relief. While they can be uncomfortable and embarrassing, I found ways to manage them. I became an expert in the art of dressing in layers! I ultimately found that prayer and exercise reduced my stress and hot flashes.

Health Risks as Hormone Levels Drop

Dropping levels of estrogen and progesterone during menopause result in increased health risks. It's essential to be aware of these risks and to take proactive measures to stay healthy.

Bone Loss and Osteoporosis

Women can lose up to 5% of their bone mass in the first five years of menopause. This loss can lead to osteoporosis, where bones become brittle and fragile. Statistics show that four in 20 women over 65 have osteoporosis, and 50% of women over 50 will break a bone because of this condition. The risk of breaking a hip is particularly concerning as it can significantly impact a woman's ability to live independently, with one in five women who break their hip dying within a year.

Rise in Heart Disease Risk

Menopause also increases the risk of heart disease. Estrogen has a protective effect on the heart, and as its levels drop, women become more susceptible to cardiovascular issues.

Sarcopenia: Loss of Muscle Mass

Sarcopenia, the loss of muscle mass, is another challenge that often accompanies menopause. This loss can lead to weight gain and decreased strength, affecting overall quality of life.

The Good News

Before throwing in the towel, let's discuss the silver lining. While the challenges of menopause can be daunting, the good news is that you can take action to counterbalance most of the decline that happens.

Being proactive about your health and having a support network will help you navigate this phase with strength and vitality.

I began my journey toward healthy living when I was 39, and my first (and only) son was born. I aimed to optimize my health so I could stay active and do fun activities with him as he grew up. When perimenopause hit in my late 40s, I had a head start on healthy living as I was already using supplements, working on improving my diet, and increasing my exercise routine. I became more determined to stay active and healthy through the menopausal cycle and reach "the other side" with vitality. I started reading books, listening to talks, and attending conferences, and ultimately, I enrolled in a health coach study program with the Institute for Integrative Nutrition.

Don't Live in Fear—My Osteoporosis Story

As I journeyed into menopause, I realized that osteoporosis was my primary health risk. I first learned that I was at risk for osteoporosis when I was in my early 40s and had a preliminary screening at a health fair. After a consult with my doctor, I had a full bone scan, which showed I had osteopenia. I adjusted my lifestyle, including my diet and exercise, to fight the progression of this condition. At 4'10", the prospect of shrinking was not attractive!

I delved into research on osteoporosis and found out I was at higher risk because I am short and not overweight! I learned that weight-bearing exercise and diet can affect my bone health. Our bone mass peaks around the age of 29. Our bones are constantly building and breaking down. The dilemma is that the breaking down part accelerates, and the building up part decelerates as we age. I became determined not to let this disease determine what I could do as I grew older.

I shifted my diet toward healthier choices with more calcium and vitamin D-rich foods crucial for bone health, like leafy greens, dairy, and fish. My diet gradually moved away from processed foods and sugar, which can contribute to bone density loss, but it went to the next level when I enrolled in a program to become a health coach. Until then, I had a pantry stocked with quinoa, whole grains, lentils, and beans, but often they got stuck on the shelf. The shift wasn't just about adding certain foods; it was about creating a balanced, nutrient-rich diet that supported my overall health and helped me manage my osteoporosis, turning a challenge into a pathway for a healthier lifestyle.

I developed a love for running in my 50s. It is now a big part of my physical and mental health routine. Besides being good for my bones, it helps me manage my stress level and has brought a new community of friends into my life.

Strength training became another essential part of my formula for healthy bones. I began going to a gym and learned how to get started without injuring myself. Now, I use YouTube videos and sometimes connect with friends via Zoom to work out together. You don't have to use heavy weights, and you don't need a lot of equipment. Light to moderate dumbbells is an excellent place to start. The important thing is to be consistent.

Part of the monitoring of my health included yearly or biennial bone scans. My osteopenia progressed to an osteoporosis diagnosis in my spine. Rather than give up, I became more diligent about my bone health plan, including diet, supplements, strength training, and weight-bearing exercise. Being in the natural health arena for many years, I resisted the idea of hormone replacement therapy and oral bisphosphonate prescription drugs. Bisphosphonate drugs inhibit the cells' activity responsible for the bone breakdown. At the time I first learned about this treatment option, it was standard practice to put someone on a never-ending prescription. I reviewed the side effects, including gastrointestinal issues, nausea, and, in rare cases, jaw osteonecrosis. I declined.

As I approached 60, I consulted with an endocrinologist to gain deeper insights into my diagnosis and treatment options. I learned I had come through the most rapid part of bone loss in the first five years after menopause. After reviewing various treatment options, I chose a once-a-year injection of a drug called Reclast for three years. After three years of treatment, my last bone scan showed my bone health had stabilized.

Rather than live in fear of this disease, I am choosing not to let it slow me down or prevent me from taking on new challenges. I continue running 10 K races and a few half marathons—something I never would have imagined doing 15 years ago. Last year, to celebrate my 65th birthday, I led a group of three women, and we went on a three-day backpacking trip to the bottom of the Grand Canyon.

Two Factors Carried Me through the Difficult Times

Besides the challenges of physical changes in my body and the emotional ups and downs of hormonal changes, I faced life situations that came close to derailing me in my perimenopausal through early menopause years. Within two years, my corporate job of 19 years laid me off at the age of 47, my mom came to live with us and passed away three months later, and my husband underwent spinal back surgery and lost his career as an RN. What followed was a period of extreme financial and emotional stress. The aftermath of these events included my husband becoming addicted to the narcotic pain medication from his surgery, many rounds of in-patient rehab, and the eventual diagnosis of bipolar disorder and disability status.

I am grateful I had two groups, plus my passion for my business, that aided me through this time and helped me grow strong. My faith community and circle of health-minded friends were the safety net that kept me afloat. Knowing I could call on my "church lady" friends for prayer support and help with my son at a moment's notice lowered my stress level. My health and wellness mentors related to my business provided me with advice on menopausal symptoms and natural remedies and supplements. My passion for helping others improve their health gave me a purpose that took my attention off my hardships and allowed me to find joy amid the turmoil.

Regardless of the health or life issues you experience during menopause, I encourage you to take an active approach to your well-being and seek out personalized solutions. Get various opinions if needed, create a support network of like-minded women, but don't give up. Your habits will determine your future health, happiness, and longevity.

Top Health Tips for Navigating Menopause

1. **Diet: Eat Real Food**

   Aim for 80% of your diet to consist of foods with one ingredient! Seven to nine servings of fresh fruits and veggies is a great goal! If you are far from this level, start with a small step. Avoid processed foods high in sugar, artificial sweeteners, and additives. Eating real food will stabilize your blood sugar levels, reduce inflammation, and provide the nutrients your body needs. Consider adding soy to your diet. It is a powerful ally in managing menopausal symptoms. It is rich in phytoestrogens, plant compounds that mimic the effects of estrogen in the body. Consuming soy products and supplements can help reduce hot flashes and improve heart health. Soy is also an excellent source of protein, making it a valuable addition to your diet.

2. **Get Adequate Protein**

   Protein plays a crucial role in building muscle and maintaining metabolism. Ensuring adequate protein intake becomes even more critical as muscle mass declines with age. Protein helps with muscle repair and growth and keeps you fuller for longer, aiding in weight management.

3. **Move That Body**

   Engaging in weight-bearing exercises is essential for maintaining bone density and increasing aerobic capacity. Walking, running, and dancing stress your bones, stimulating them to become stronger. Include some balance exercises to help prevent falls and injuries, especially as we age. Find an activity you love. Aim to do it 3–5 times a week. Seek to improve your Vo2 Max, the maximum amount of oxygen your body can utilize during intense exercise. A higher Vo2 Max is associated with a stronger, more efficient heart and lungs and a lower risk of chronic disease. Improving your Vo2 Max can help you live a longer, more vibrant life.

4. **Get Strong—Build Muscle to Maintain Your Metabolism**

   Maintaining and building muscle mass is vital for bone health and metabolism. Muscles provide support and stability to your bones, reducing the risk of fractures and osteoporosis. Muscle burns more calories at rest when compared to fat. Building and maintaining muscle mass will boost your metabolism and make it easier to stay at a healthy weight. Aim for three times a week.

5. **Snooze to Win—Prioritize Sleep Like It's Your Job**

   Sleep aids in recovery, regulates hormones, and supports cognitive function. Go to bed and get up at the same time each day, make your room dark and comfortably cool, and unplug from technology at least an hour before bedtime.

6. **Seek Professional Support if Needed**

   Don't hesitate to seek professional support if you need it. Consulting with healthcare providers, nutritionists, fitness experts, and mental health professionals can provide valuable guidance and support.

7. **Cultivating Gratitude**

   Gratitude is an essential tool for finding joy and contentment in life. Keep a gratitude journal, practice daily affirmations, and remember to show appreciation to the people who enrich your life.

8. **Seek Harmony**

   Incorporate prayer, meditation, and breathing exercises into your routine so that the song of your daily life is a happy tune, even through the challenges you face through menopause and beyond.

9. **Find Your Tribe**

   Seek women your age and older who can share their wisdom and experiences with you. Find a support group or start your own! The friendly accountability of a group can make the difference between reading about what to do and implementing these strategies into your daily habits! Strong social ties lead to a longer, happier life.

10. **Live a Life of Purpose**

    When you have a cause that you are passionate about, it helps to take your focus off your hardships.

The Great, Exciting, Empowering, and Liberating News

Menopause is not the end of your vibrant life, but a new chapter. Have a positive, open mindset, and you can turn it into an opportunity to grow, learn new skills, reconnect with long-time friends, make new ones, embark on adventures, and volunteer. I call my approach to this stage of life—Living Younger Longer. I don't believe our age should define who we are, what we can do, and who we are becoming.

Caring for Yourself So You Can Serve Others

The energy and focus you spent raising your family can now be funneled into taking care of yourself (physically, mentally, and spiritually) so you can give back to your community. My mission is to inspire women over 50 to become their healthiest selves so they can best serve others. My motto is to Be More—become the best version of yourself, Make More—more connections, more of an impact, and more income, so I can ultimately Give More of my time, talent, and treasure to others.

Building Resilience

Life beyond menopause may bring its share of difficulties, but it also offers a chance to cultivate resilience. Building resilience allows you to adapt to change and bounce back from challenges. My husband's health has continued to decline, and he now has chronic lung disease and cannot travel or even participate in many family, church, or social activities. There are not too many activities that we can engage in together. So I relish the simple things like cooking together or watching a movie. Some days, it's challenging to cope with, but I have chosen not to let this reality stop me from engaging in activities I love. I've created a network of friends who are my travel, hiking, running, cooking, and faith buddies. Whether we are attending a local cultural or church event, walking or running locally, or traveling for an adventure or a conference, I've been able to let go of the fear of what might happen to my husband while I am away from home.

Put the Power of Positivity to Work

You don't have to look far today to find positive mindset gurus who will advise that the thoughts you focus on and the emotions you entertain each day will determine your reality, your life, and who you become. Behind all the clever motivational quotes, there lies a science of positive psychology that shows nurturing an attitude of gratitude, happiness, and joy results in an improved outcome in all areas of your life. Put this knowledge into practice during this menopausal stage of life, and you can make it the best chapter ever.

What You Think, You Look.
What You Think, You Do.
What You Think, You Are!
—Dr. Forrest C. Shaklee

Menopause is a new beginning—a time to redefine your life with strength, balance, and joy. Embrace the wisdom, resilience, and joy, and live each day with purpose and passion. My 66th birthday celebration this year included a 21.5-mile hike/run around a lakefront path with a friend. We stumbled upon a quote a homeowner painted on a fence for all the hikers. It sums up my outlook for the future.

"What a wonderful thought it is that some of the best days of our lives haven't happened yet."

I strive to make each day a "best day." Want to join me?

Scan the QR code to learn more about my approach to healthy living and schedule a Living Younger Longer health chat.

References

- Strong Women, Strong Bones - Miriam Nelson
- Outlive - Dr. Peter Attia
- Slaying the supplement myths - Dr. Steve Chaney
- The Blue Zones Solution - Dan Buettner
- The Happiness Advantage - Shawn Achor
- Reflections on a Philosophy - Dr. Forrest C. Shaklee

Kim Rendon

The Menopause Rebel
Registered Dietitian

https://www.linkedin.com/in/kimrendon/
https://www.facebook.com/kim.rendon.31392
https://www.instagram.com/the.menopause.rebel/
https://menopause-rebel.com

Kim is a seasoned Registered Dietitian with over 30 years of experience who has transitioned into health coaching and gut health practice. She specializes in working with the "Menopause Rebels"— inviting women to embrace their rebellious spirits and embark on a transformative journey through menopause. Kim's approach combines her extensive nutritional knowledge with a deep understanding of gut health, offering a holistic perspective on wellness during midlife transitions.

Balancing a full-time career while raising two athletic sons, Kim navigated her own perimenopause journey while her children went through puberty. This unique experience has enriched her professional insights, allowing her to relate personally to the challenges faced by her clients.

With her wealth of experience and empathetic approach, Kim is dedicated to empowering women to embrace their menopausal journey. She focuses on gut health as a cornerstone of overall well-being, demonstrating her passion for helping her clients achieve their health goals.

I Thought I Was Having a Heart Attack!

By Kim Rendon

Perimenopause?

I hadn't even heard of such a thing.

When I started having hot flashes, I thought I was in menopause. But it wasn't until I started looking into menopause that I discovered there is a whole journey to get to actual menopause. Menopause is really only one day, the day you have gone 12 months without a period.

Perimenopause is the transition leading to menopause. It is the decline of the ovaries as they begin to produce less estrogen and progesterone. That is when all the fun begins!

I had my boys in my mid-30s, which meant I was going through perimenopause at the same time as they were going through puberty. Perimenopause is just puberty in reverse. You can only imagine the raging hormones and moodiness that were in that household.

In my early 40s, I had a uterine ablation because my periods were becoming very heavy. An ablation is a medical procedure where they go in and cauterize the uterine lining. What a relief it was to no longer have periods. But the one thing that never crossed my mind was the fact that even though I didn't have a period, I still did the whole monthly cycling thing, still having the monthly hormonal shifts. There were no irregular periods to take note of to see the transition happening.

Both of my boys were active and three-sport athletes. During this time, I worked full time, ran them to practices and games, was on the Christian education board at church, was vice president of the athletic boosters, and ran concession stands for games. I was tired and overwhelmed. Some days, I didn't know what direction I was going.

Sometimes, meals were thrown together for a quick meal or eaten on the run. Think hot dogs, popcorn, and Mt Dew in the bleachers of whatever sporting event we were at. And I would often think, "I'm a dietitian, and I'm eating like this? But it was more about survival at that moment.

Along with the overwhelm and the exhaustion, depression began to happen. Some days, it felt like I couldn't keep it together and couldn't think straight. I experienced brain fog or forgot what I was saying in the middle of it all. I figured this was just life.

The depression worsened after my son left for the Marine Corps. I felt like I was in a big black void and was too tired to try and crawl out of it. I tried several different antidepressants without success. Instead, I medicated with food, causing a lot of weight gain. And then I just felt worse. Along with all of this came high blood pressure and cholesterol. I was put on medication for the blood pressure but refused meds for cholesterol.

Then, one morning, I woke up in the early morning with a sharp pain. It wasn't really in my chest, but I didn't quite know what to think about it. I knew the signs of heart attack in women are different than in men. But when I looked it up, what I was experiencing wasn't what was described, but who knew? I never experience things the way the symptoms are supposed to be.

I sat there trying to decide whether to go to the ER or wait to see if the pain went away. What if it really was a heart attack, though? Waiting around wouldn't be good. Then, there was the issue of how I would get there. Drive myself? Call an ambulance? My seventeen-year-old son was the only other person in the house, and I didn't want to ask him to drive his mom to the ER.

I ended up calling my ex-husband to take me to the hospital. Once there, all the standard tests were run, and I was eventually diagnosed with dyspepsia and esophagitis. Basically, it was indigestion and inflammation of the esophagus from an acid burn.

It was the beginning of the pandemic, and being the people person, the one who loved to get hugs and have personal contact, I was feeling lonely, isolated, depressed, and every other emotion we were all feeling at that time. The night before the incident, I sent my son out to get fast food burgers, fries, and Cokes. I don't typically eat all that, but I was eating my feelings. Even though I went to bed hours after eating, I still had a stomach full of food. Some of the food and acid flowed back into my esophagus while I slept, causing esophagitis.

I had already been experiencing a lot of heartburn/indigestion over the past couple of years and consumed a lot of antacids. Many times, I was waking in the night to get up and chew on some antacids so that I could go back to sleep. Now, I was being put on prescription antacids. In the beginning, I needed it while my esophagus was healing, but eventually, it made me feel full all of the time, and I was even more miserable.

What I didn't know was that this is part of perimenopause. The indigestion, heartburn, bloating, gas, constipation, and diarrhea were all part of this grand journey I was on.

Were you surprised to know that digestive issues were related to perimenopause? I was. There are many signs or symptoms that tell us we are on the menopause journey. I've seen it said that there are upwards of 80 different signs. Many of them I have experienced, but I just put them up as being stressed and overwhelmed by my crazy life with teenage boys. And, actually, being easily stressed and overwhelmed is part of it.

Just a few of the signs are…

- Heart palpitations
- Joint and muscle pain

- Flare-up of arthritis
- New or worsening of chronic illnesses and autoimmune diseases
- Vertigo
- High cholesterol and high triglycerides
- Headaches or migraines
- Incontinence
- Loss of muscle tone
- Memory challenges and brain fog
- Anxiety, depression, and panic attack
- Itchy ears
- Bloating
- Brittle nails
- Body odor
- Fatigue
- Urinary tract infections

We don't experience all of them. Each woman's menopause experience is different.

However, when we have one of these symptoms, traditional medicine often treats symptoms in isolation, sending us from one specialist to another. But we're more than a collection of symptoms. We're whole beings - mind, body, and spirit interconnected. It's time to embrace a holistic approach to menopause. This means addressing not just physical symptoms but also our emotional well-being and spiritual health. By treating ourselves as complete individuals, we can find balanced, comprehensive solutions that nurture every aspect of our being. Let's redefine menopause care to honor our whole selves and promote true healing.

Unfortunately, many doctors, even gynecologists, lack comprehensive training in menopause care. Too often, women's concerns are dismissed or minimized, with practitioners claiming there's nothing wrong or that we should simply endure these changes. This dismissive attitude can leave us feeling devalued and invisible. It's time we demand better understanding and care for our menopausal journey. We deserve to be heard, validated, and offered real solutions during this significant life transition.

I finally reached a point where I decided I couldn't do this anymore. I didn't want to feel this way. That's when I began my health journey. I started seeing a naturopath practitioner who has put it all together and treats the root of what is causing the issues rather than treating the symptoms. From there, I started a gut-healing journey.

Are you thinking, "What does healing your gut have to do with it?"

Well, let me tell you about it. The health of your gut is the root of many issues we deal with in our health, immunity, and mental health. Years of eating a diet of highly processed foods filled with sugar, high-stress lifestyles, and living life on the edge affect the health of your gut. Add declining estrogen to it, and it goes from bad to worse.

And here is what has happened along the way.

Diet:

I started by decreasing the amount of sugar I was eating. My naturopath had me write down everything I ate and circle everything that contained sugar. Sugar in any form. Have you ever looked at where sugar is added to food? It is in some of the craziest foods.

Once I started healing my gut, along with the sugar, I removed processed foods, gluten, dairy, soy, and corn. While it was tough letting go of these foods, I found a new freedom in how I felt. I experienced less brain fog, more energy, and weight loss, and many of my allergy symptoms disappeared.

Manage stress:

As our estrogen and progesterone levels drop, our stress hormone, cortisol, becomes more dominant. This makes us more prone to stress and anxiety during menopause. Learning stress management tools is important.

A couple of my tools:

- Taking some time to stop and consciously breathe
- Meditating
- Self-care
- Sitting in nature

Prioritize sleep:

Sleep is where our bodies are doing their best to heal and rejuvenate. We need 7 to 9 hours of quality sleep, but it can be so hard sometimes to get it. A couple of tips to help with getting a good sleep:

- Set up a bedtime routine at the same time every night, whether washing your face and brushing your teeth, taking a warm bath with lavender, or reading, meditating, or journaling.
- Shut off electronics at least an hour before bed.
- Don't eat less than 3 hours before going to bed. And a big hint: Sugar and alcohol make hot flashes/night sweats more intense.

Movement:

Getting some form of joyful movement most days of the week. Something that feels good to you that you want to do. I love to have an 80s dance party right in my living room all by myself. Remember to add in strength training. Declining estrogen also means we lose muscle mass.

Deal with past hurts and traumas:

Addressing past hurts and traumas is crucial for your overall health because unresolved emotional issues can create chronic stress, negatively impacting your body's functions through the mind-body connection. By healing emotionally, you can improve your overall well-being, leading to better lifestyle choices and self-care practices that support your health throughout life's transitions. For me, this is a continued work in progress.

Some forms of healing are:

- Talk therapy
- Mindfulness meditation
- Journaling
- Cognitive Behavior Therapy (CBT)
- EMDR (Eye Movement Desensitization and Reprocessing)
- Breathwork
- Body-focused (somatic) therapies: These are methods that use physical sensations and movements to help understand and heal emotional issues. They believe that our bodies hold important clues about our mental health.

You can use several of these at the same time. There is no magic formula. It's all about what works for you. For me, I like to do somatic work, and when things come up, I can take those back to my counselor to unpack what is happening there.

So, it's time to shake up traditional menopause approaches, take back our power, and become menopause rebels. As menopause rebels, we defy the stereotypes and negative connotations often associated with menopause, challenge the idea that menopause is something to be ashamed of or hidden, and celebrate the wisdom, strength, and resilience that come with age and life experience.

I recommend beginning to keep a journal of your different symptoms, track your periods, do a little research, and have a list of questions. Make an appointment with your health care practitioner or gynecologist and have an open conversation with them to see what help you can get.

Here are my top 5 recommendations for redefining your menopause experience so you can keep living your best life as you traverse the menopause journey and beyond:

1. Purpose/Purposeful Life:

Discovering and pursuing your purpose during menopause can profoundly impact your overall well-being. When you have a clear sense of purpose, you're more likely to engage in activities that bring you joy, fulfillment, and meaning. This can help reduce stress and promote a more positive outlook on life, which can, in turn, have a ripple effect on your physical health.

2. The Right Foods:

Fueling your body with the right foods is crucial for feeling your best during menopause. Focus on a nutrient-dense, whole-food diet rich in fiber, prebiotics, probiotics, and anti-inflammatory foods that can enhance your body's resilience and vitality during this transitional phase.

3. Movement with a Purpose:

Engaging in movement with a purpose during menopause is a powerful way to promote overall well-being. When you choose physical activities that align with your interests, values, and goals, you're more likely to experience joy, satisfaction, and a sense of accomplishment, which can positively impact your mental and emotional state.

4. Spirituality:

Embracing spirituality during menopause can profoundly foster a deep sense of connection, purpose, and inner peace. Engaging in spiritual practices that resonate with you, such as meditation, prayer, mindfulness, or connecting with nature, can help reduce stress, cultivate self-awareness, and promote a greater sense of harmony between your mind, body, and spirit.

5. Community or Tribe:

Surrounding yourself with a supportive community or tribe during menopause impacts your overall health. When you have a network of like-minded individuals who understand and validate your experiences, you can feel more connected, empowered, and resilient in the face of challenges. This sense of belonging and social support can help reduce stress, improve mood, and foster a greater sense of well-being.

Jesse Schewchuk

CEO of Modern Muse Media

https://www.linkedin.com/feed/
https://www.facebook.com/jesseschewchuk/
https://www.instagram.com/msjessemuse/
https://modernmusemedia.ca/
https://www.themenopausemission.org/

Multi-award-winning Television Producer Jesse Schewchuk is the Founder and CEO of a thriving Content Creation Training Agency, Modern Muse Media. A natural storyteller with over two decades of television experience, Jesse is now focused on helping industry professionals build their brand awareness with intention and capitalize on the tangible impact of video as the premier medium for business promotion and marketing. Her achievements led to a Cover Feature in Avenue Magazine's "Top 40 under 40" and the Entrepreneur of the Year Award (Business from the Heart 2022). Jesse is currently the President of The Menopause Mission, a non-profit she founded in 2023, Past-President of the Edmonton Business Association, Past Vice-President of Women In Film & Television of Alberta, and Director of Communications for Synergy Network. Her passion is contagious and her vision is to educate, empower and elevate people through the power of authenticity, story, and content creation every single day.

It Came In Like A Wrecking Ball

By Jesse Schewchuk

Staring up at the ceiling, I felt like I had been lying there forever. The room was dark, the blinds drawn tight to block out the world. A few rays of light crept through the edges, but they did nothing to lift the oppressive weight that had settled on me. I had been in bed for two days, crying relentlessly, unable to stop the tears. They just kept coming, wave after wave, without any sign of relief. The last time I had cried this hard was when my mother died in my arms all those years ago.

But this was different. This pain wasn't physical; it wasn't tied to a specific loss. It was mental, emotional—like a heavy cloud that had enveloped me completely, making it hard to breathe, hard to think. I found myself contemplating the unthinkable. Maybe I would go into the garage, start the car, and just let the engine run. Or perhaps I'd drive down the highway, and I'd simply veer off and turn into an oncoming semi-truck. Anything to make this pain go away because living like this didn't seem worth it anymore.

I wasn't scared of dying. What terrified me was the feeling that I was losing my mind. It's probably the scariest feeling in the world, to feel like your grip on reality is slipping away. I didn't know it at the time, but what I was experiencing was menopause. And it had come for me like a wrecking ball.

Rewind almost ten years earlier, and I was at the height of my career. I was an award-winning television producer, and my name appeared in all the right places. After eighteen years of working my way up from the bottom, I had finally reached the top. My career was everything to me. It was my identity, my purpose, and I was willing to sacrifice anything to maintain that. It was what I distracted myself with to not have to deal with the gaping hole in my heart that was the loss of my mother to breast cancer.

I had always been driven by a need to prove myself, a fire that burned inside me for as long as I could remember. There's something intoxicating about being the best at what you do, about achieving a level of success that others only dream about. And in many ways, I was living that dream.

Even after my daughter was born, I would sacrifice moments with her, missing out on small, precious moments of her childhood because I was too busy striving for my next goal. I missed bedtime stories, family dinners, and even those little moments when she just wanted to sit and watch a show together. I was too consumed by my own ambition to notice that the most valuable things were slipping through my fingers. To this day, that is hard to admit, but it is true.

And then there was my health—sacrificed on more occasions than I can count. I was on the front cover of Avenue Magazine's prestigious Top 40 Under 40 list. I walked red carpets, met celebrities, wore custom gowns, and was even nominated for the Canadian equivalent of an Emmy. But none of that mattered in the grand scheme of things. All the accolades and success were gained at the expense of my own well-being. I didn't realize it at the time, but I was slowly burning out. The problem with burnout is that it sneaks up on you. You don't notice it until you're completely consumed by it until it's too late to reverse the damage.

When we finished filming the fifth and final season of the television show I had been working on, it marked the end of my career in television. I didn't leave because I wanted to; I left because I had no choice. After spending my entire career in TV, I struggled to find work anywhere else. No one would hire me because they saw me as a one-trick pony. I had only ever worked in one industry, and to them, that meant I had nothing to offer outside of it.

The rejection was a punch to the gut. It was as if all my hard work, all the years I'd spent building a name for myself, had been for nothing. But I refused to give up. That same drive that had pushed me to the top of my career was still alive, and it pushed me to start my own business. It was the logical next step. I had all these skills from producing TV, and I figured I could use them to help businesses create videos for their own brands. I knew I had something to prove. I had always been ambitious, always driven by the need to succeed, and failure wasn't an option.

But running a business turned out to be much harder than I ever imagined. I thought managing a cast and crew of 500 on a TV show was tough, but that was nothing compared to entrepreneurship. Running your own business requires an entirely different skill set. It's not just about being good at what you do; it's about wearing a million different hats, juggling client needs, financial management, marketing, and more—all while dealing with the pressure of keeping your head above water. But I was starting to drown...

The pressure to succeed mounted, and soon, I found myself in the hospital—not once, but twice—for burnout and pneumonia. My body was giving me every signal that it couldn't keep going like this, but I ignored the red flags. I pushed forward because that's what I'd always done. I didn't know how to stop. I had to keep going, had to prove myself. I remember having a conversation with my dad who asked me, "Jesse, where is the line?" There wasn't one. Looking back now, I see that all those years of overworking, neglecting my health, and ignoring my own needs were what led me to early-onset menopause.

Some women experience perimenopause over a span of ten years, with symptoms gradually creeping in, some women barely notice anything at all. I now know, there are more than sixty signs and symptoms associated with (peri)menopause, but for me, it all happened so suddenly. It felt like a wrecking ball had come crashing into my life, knocking me off my feet and stealing all of my joy. I couldn't recognize myself anymore. All the things that had once made me happy felt distant and unattainable. I was living, but I wasn't alive.

In hindsight, the signs had been there all along. There were probably small changes in my body and mood that I just ignored because I was too focused on everything else. That's what we, as women, do. We put on the proverbial cape, keep our heads down, and go, go, go—until we hit a wall. And that wall hit me hard. Think of a video of safety testing a vehicle and I was the crash test dummy.

It wasn't until I found myself lying in that bed, staring at that ceiling, contemplating whether I wanted to live or die, that I finally understood what was happening to me. My doctor had taken blood tests months earlier and found elevated levels of FSH, which is a clear indicator of menopause. But I didn't pay much attention to it at the time. I had stopped having periods, but that didn't seem like a big deal. In fact, it felt like a blessing not to have to deal with the hassle of menstruation anymore.

But that day in June of 2022, everything came crashing down. I was in bed, crying uncontrollably for two days straight when my daughter came into the room. She sat down beside me, placed her hand on my back, and asked, "Mommy, do I need to call someone?" That was the moment I realized I needed help. That I needed to call someone. I couldn't keep doing this on my own.

Asking for help has never been easy for me. I've always prided myself on being strong, independent, and capable of handling anything life throws at me. But this was different. This wasn't something I could just power through. I needed to figure out what was going on with my body and why I felt like I was losing control.

My doctor had already put me on the waiting list for the menopause clinic, but there was no telling when I would get in. I knew I couldn't wait. I needed answers, and I needed them fast. So, I made an appointment with my naturopath. We ran a series of tests, including a Dutch test and more blood work, to get to the root of what was happening.

The results were staggering. I wasn't just going through menopause; I was completely depleted on a mitochondrial level. My body was in a state of burnout so severe that it was affecting every aspect of my mental and physical health. It was evident that to address the severe menopause symptoms, we needed to treat the burnout and cellular depletion.

It turns out that menopause isn't just about the loss of reproductive function. It's about a total hormonal shift, one that impacts your brain, your heart, your muscles—every part of you. I learned that estrogen, progesterone, and testosterone all play critical roles in maintaining not just reproductive health, but mental clarity, emotional stability, and physical energy. The sudden drop in these hormones can feel like your body is betraying you.

I thought menopause would just mean hot flashes and the end of periods. In fact, in my family, it was often a joke met with rolled eyeballs and a total lack of empathy. I remember hearing things like, "Crack the windows or Auntie is going to melt." And everyone would laugh. But it was so much more. I experienced brain fog so thick it felt like I was constantly walking through a haze. Simple tasks, like remembering what I needed to pick up from the grocery store or finding my keys and my phone became impossible. I couldn't articulate well or even finish sentences. My moods were all over the place. One minute I was fine, the next I was in tears for no apparent reason. And then, there was the RAGE. The hot flashes were unbearable, coming at the most inconvenient times and drenching me in sweat. I would lie awake at night, unable to sleep, my mind racing with anxiety.

But the worst part was the emotional toll. I felt like I was losing myself, like the woman I had always been was slipping away, and there was nothing I could do to stop it. It was a profound sense of loss—loss of control, identity, and joy.

My naturopath put me on a regimen of weekly IV treatments to replenish my body at a cellular level. Slowly but surely, I started to feel better. It wasn't an overnight transformation, but over time, I began to experience small improvements. I started to feel more like myself again, though I knew I would never be the same as I was before. This experience had changed me in ways I couldn't yet fully understand.

And that's when I realized something important: I didn't have to go through this alone. There's a huge stigma around menopause, a sense that it's something we shouldn't talk about, something we should just push through quietly. But that's not how it should be. We need to have open conversations about menopause. We need to share our experiences and support one another through this life-altering transition so I started talking about it. The more I talked about it, the more women spoke up and confessed their experiences. It was at that point that it became extremely obvious that there was a huge gap. Women were being dismissed, misinformed, and disempowered.

I decided to launch a non-profit called The Menopause Mission because I wanted to create a space for women to come together and talk about what they're going through and connect with educators and experts who would listen to and guide them. It's not just about providing information, though that's a big part of it. It's about building a community where women feel safe to share their struggles and victories. Too many women suffer in silence, believing that they're the only ones feeling this way.

I never wanted to go through menopause, let alone talk about it publicly. But now that I've been through it, I see that it's a crucial part of the conversation around women's health. Menopause isn't just about getting older; it's about entering a new phase of life, one that can be empowering if we approach it the right way. But first, we have to stop pretending it's not happening. We have to break the stigma and start talking about it.

I wouldn't have chosen this path, but I've learned so much about myself along the way. The most important lesson? We need to listen to our bodies. I will never again push myself to the point of burnout. We live in a culture that glorifies the hustle, but we have to take care of ourselves first. Our bodies give us signals, and if we ignore them, we end up paying the price.

The answers are there if we're willing to stop, listen, and ask for help. I'm living proof of that. I'm stronger now than I've ever been, not because I pushed through, but because I learned to slow down and take care of myself. And now, I'm committed to helping other women do the same.

Through The Menopause Mission, I hope to inspire other women to prioritize their health, ask for help when they need it, and understand that they're not alone in this journey. Together, we can rise, stronger, and more empowered than ever before and make this "M" word mainstream.

Jane Butler

Founder and CEO of Individually You Coaching
Womens Health and Wellness Coach,

https://www.facebook.com/groups/loveyourmenopausewithjane/
https://www.instagram.com/individually.you/
www.individuallyyoucoaching.com
www.aloeshopwithjane.com

Jane Butler, MSc, is a former UK Registered Nurse and Consultant Nurse for Heart Failure with over 4 decades of experience in the NHS. Now a certified Health Coach specializing in women's health, Jane is a dedicated advocate for menopause awareness, empowering women with the latest information and support. She is the founder and CEO of "Individually You Coaching," offering personalized lifestyle approaches to help women thrive in the next chapter of their lives. Having experienced insomnia during her own menopause transition, Jane is passionate about helping women overcome sleep problems. She embraces a "back to basics" approach to problem-solving as the foundation of her coaching methodology. Jane balances her professional passion with her roles as a wife, mother, and grandmother, and she splits her time between the UK and California. Her interests include cooking, reading, traveling and family. Join her in her "Love your menopause with Jane" Facebook group.

Embracing Change:
My Journey Through Menopause

By Jane Butler

From Nurse to Health Coach: A Personal Tale of Strength, Balance, and Joy

After over four decades as a UK Registered Nurse, I thought I had seen it all. But nothing prepared me for menopause. I'm embarrassed to even mention that I had NEVER EVER heard the term "perimenopause"!!! That's ridiculous I hear you say – it's everywhere you turn these days. You can't miss it. Maybe so, but just ten years ago, that was not the case.

I can confirm that as I write this, I am very much 'post-menopausal' and feel vibrant and liberated. I am the most comfortable and confident that I have ever been and attribute it to the life experiences, awareness, and intelligence I have gathered over my lifetime. Someone once said that menopause was the other bookend to puberty, which when you think about it, for us women, totally makes sense. In my teens, I felt like I was unstoppable but never had the resources to make that a reality, in my 20s, I felt the need to keep up with others, and in my 30s, the need to prove myself. In my 40s, it was all about maintenance (as the hormonal roller-coaster left the station) and in my 50s … well, that's another story.

I got through the perimenopause stage alone, confused, and without the support that would have saved me and those around me a lot of frustration, grief, and even despair. Having traveled this path alone confused, frightened, and feeling like I was in early dementia and "cuckoo" for sure, it's my mission, that those of you following behind, have a hugely better- and well-informed experience. That you get to take control because you understand what is happening, know where to go for support and advice, and see this next stage as the real opportunity it can be, should you choose.

My symptoms started subtly in my late forties, with a little tiredness but I put that down to having started a new job as a Consultant Nurse – a position I had worked hard for and wanted to be a huge success at, so I was throwing myself into it in every way I could think of: networking, showing up everywhere I thought mattered and continuing to educate myself. To this end, I was studying for my master's degree and travelling one day a week to Brighton University for lectures. As a wife and a mother of two teenage children, I thought, "Well, it's obvious I'd be tired, right?" However, it got to the point where I decided to see my family doctor just in case, I needed to top up my iron as I also noticed my periods were getting heavy. After a blood test, my doctor said I had an under-active thyroid and that was the cause – made sense to me and I started on Levothyroxine and sure enough I felt better – problem solved I thought. No further doctor visits.

Life was great for a while, and I was getting a great buzz out of my career and loved studying. Again, my periods rose their ugly head – they got really heavy. I mean with large clots and flooding. At first, I found ways to manage them, and then when I got so fed up with them, I went back to see my family doctor. This time a blood test showed I was extremely low with my hemoglobin (iron) so low that it was suggested to admit me for a blood transfusion. I was wholly against that due to my busy schedule, so it was decided to start me on iron tablets and a medication to stop my periods and make an appointment to have a Mirena coil fitted (which I learned would regulate or totally stop my periods, however, my doctor couldn't tell me which). As yet nothing had been mentioned about menopause, let alone 'perimenopause'.

Soon enough, mood swings and relentless fatigue appeared and became my new normal. Insomnia, though, was the worst. Night after night, I found myself wide awake, counting sheep that never brought sleep.

The exhaustion seeped into every part of my life, affecting work, relationships, and my well-being. There was one night when, after hours of restless tossing and turning, I decided to get up out of bed and go downstairs and bake. Well, why not? Seemed like a great idea at the time.

Kneading that dough in the quiet of my kitchen, I found a strange sense of calm. I can still feel the dough in my hands now thinking back to that night. While making that bread, I discovered that small, soothing activities could ease my anxiety and frustration versus lying in bed tossing and turning at 3 am every morning. Well, the upside was I had a lot of fresh bread available for breakfast the following mornings – a small win, I guess! (I have shared my bread recipe at the end of the chapter for you to try out, hopefully not at 3 am, though!!!)

At this point, another doctor visit brought up the topic of 'menopause'. Hmm, I thought – "How long is this going to go on for, doctor?" I asked. "Who knows," he said, "Possibly a few months, maybe ten years."

WHAT, ten years? WTF!!! This guy must be nuts I thought. He doesn't know what he is talking about – ten years, who would have this and not do anything about it. "Yes, my dear, it's just something you ladies have to put up with." No explanation, no education, no referral elsewhere, and very definitely no mention of the word 'perimenopause'. I walked out of there shocked and bewildered. Ok, well, this won't happen to me (my stubbornness coming out).

Despite my medical background, I felt lost. It wasn't until I began researching that I discovered "perimenopause." The revelation was both shocking and liberating. Armed with this new knowledge, I embarked on a journey to reclaim my health and happiness.

However, one of the most significant changes during this time was being made redundant (my hospital Trust was undergoing a major financial restructuring where many of the Consultant Nurse posts were dissolved as being too expensive to maintain) and my move from London to California. These major life transitions added another layer of complexity. The new environment, with its different culture and climate, provided both opportunities and challenges but at this point, I only wanted to see the challenges.

It was now that the emotional 'roller-coaster' took off with me firmly strapped in for the ride of my life, without my consent and not having agreed to buy a ticket!!!

Friends and family thought it was an amazing opportunity to move to California (so did I on my good days), but I would wake up some days in tears, feeling lost and without purpose, desperate and struggling to get out of bed. In my rational moments, I figured it was because of my redundancy, move to another country, and loss of family and friends around me, but I got really frightened because it seemed so disproportional. Anything and nothing would send me into sobs, and I got even more frustrated because I knew it was upsetting for my husband and daughter to see me like this and struggle with what to do with me. They both tried hard, but I could see the irritation at times of "just pull yourself together." My husband was kind and tried hard to understand but resorted to heading off to work to get out of it and my daughter was an absolute star and would take control, "Mum, get up, get showered, and put your makeup on, I'm taking you out," she would say. Honestly, it took such an effort and cajoling to get me out but once I was out, the world would take on another view. Thank you so much, Sarah, for getting me through those awful days.

Truthfully, it wasn't until I looked back and realized that while there were some very real reasons for feeling low and off, the reality was the 'perimenopausal' phase I was in. I considered myself educated but had only thought of menopause as "hot flushes." I now know there are over one hundred symptoms associated with the menopause transition.

Some are so subtle and attributed to many other reasons that it is often hard to pinpoint that it is connected to this time of our lives.

Eventually, the sunshine and natural beauty of California became a source of solace and inspiration, helping me find a new sense of balance and peace. It was at this time I decided to study and get certified as a Health Coach. I figured I could use my years of nursing experience along with my newfound skills of coaching to help other women going through the menopausal journey. Help them in a way that I would have loved to have available to me so that I didn't feel so alone and could see the way forward. I knew I had made the right decision after hearing of a friend who had committed suicide because of a deep depression and inability to cope with her menopausal journey and lack of effective support.

I honestly believe the key to turning things around was first to understand and accept where I was at, in perimenopause. To be aware of what was going on in my body and once I understood that I got to do something about it. By that I mean, once I knew what was happening, I could take doable and positive steps to make things better. For me (and I subsequently believe it is the same for most women) getting better control of my sleep was the foundation for getting to grips with all the other stuff. Let me be clear though, it doesn't all get resolved overnight (excuse the pun here). What I mean is that it takes time and consistency to bring about the change.

In my quest to overcome insomnia, I explored various strategies (better options than bread baking in the middle of the night). Here are some practical tips that worked for me:

1. **Establish a Routine**: Going to bed and waking up at the same time every day helped regulate my body clock. There is a ton of research and evidence to support this practice and I can promise that if you stick at it, you will see an improvement.

2. **Create a Calm Environment**: I transformed my bedroom into a peaceful retreat, free of electronic devices and distractions. This was possibly the most difficult as I had resorted to watching television for most of the night when I woke (I had got fed up with baking at this point), so removing the TV from the bedroom felt like my lifeline was being severed. To be honest I did try and sneak in my iPad at times or go out to the living room to put the TV on some nights (so I know all the sneaky things my coaching clients get up to – I did them too!!!).

3. **Mindfulness and Meditation**: Practicing mindfulness techniques before bed calmed my mind. Guided meditations became a nightly ritual. This really helped with the 'monkey brain' you know all that chatter that goes on in your head in the quietness of the middle of the night or even as you are trying to drift off. There are so many forms of meditation so please try them out until you find what works for you.

4. **Herbal Teas**: I discovered the soothing effects of chamomile and lavender teas, which helped ease me into sleep. Truthfully, at first, I didn't like the taste of any of the teas. I had been used to coffee and sugary drinks (yes, cocktails and wine included), so it was about retraining my tastebuds. Honestly, it does take time, but it is possible. Think back to your first alcoholic drink or first cigarette (if you have ever indulged in any of these activities), you didn't immediately like them – you stuck at it to "fit in" and be "accepted" by your group of friends. Trying new things like herbal teas can be viewed similarly but instead of doing it to fit in, your aim is to improve your sleep!

Gradually, I started sleeping soundly, and with restful nights came the energy and clarity I had been missing.

During this time, humor became a crucial coping mechanism. Sharing funny moments with friends and family lightened the load. I had read

about 'knicker magnets' or for my American buddies 'pantie magnets'!!!
I know what you are thinking – me too – "What the heck are they?" A
little research enlightened me to the fact that these little magnets were
placed at the front of your knickers (panties) to "create an equilibrium
to the autonomic nervous system to help minimize various symptoms
of menopause." Well, for me, the only thing they helped with was
collecting loose paper clips!!!

One evening, I was in the kitchen, fanning myself furiously because of
a hot flush. My husband walked in, saw me standing in front of the
open fridge, and said, "Trying to cool down or contemplating a
midnight snack?" This made us giggle, realizing how ridiculous
menopause could make everyday life seem.

During another hot flush moment while I was cooking dinner one
evening, my husband, sensing the impending chaos, suggested we eat
in the backyard. The thought came to mind of us dragging the dining
table outside and my husband swatting away bugs while I enjoyed the
cool evening breeze. This made me smile and lifted the mood – what
would the neighbors think if we actually took our dining room table
outside?! what could have been a meltdown moment turned into a
moment of shared laughter.

Rekindling my passions played a crucial role in this transition. I
reconnected with things I used to enjoy. Taking up reading again –
enjoying a good book just for the fun of it, getting back to the gym and
even talking my hubby into trying out some dance lessons
(unfortunately the dance lessons didn't last for too long). These
activities brought fun, joy, and a sense of accomplishment, helping me
to pay attention to parts of myself that I had neglected.

Here are some ways to rekindle passions, find a new balance in daily
life, and help reduce symptoms:

1. **Stay Active**: Engage in regular physical activity. It doesn't have
    to be strenuous; even a daily walk can make a difference.

2. **Healthy Eating**: Focus on a balanced diet rich in fruits, vegetables, and whole grains. Avoid caffeine and alcohol, especially close to bedtime – it keeps you awake and encourages hot flushes. Avoid as much 'junk food' as possible as it really does mess with your hormones!

3. **Stay Connected**: Don't isolate yourself. Talk to friends, join support groups, and share your experiences. We have treated menopause as a 'taboo' subject for way too long keeping us isolated, fearful, and uneducated.

4. **Pursue Passions**: Revisit hobbies and interests that bring you joy. Whatever you choose, activities can provide a great emotional boost and often help us stay connected.

5. **Seek Professional Help**: Don't hesitate to consult healthcare providers for advice and support. If you are not finding the support initially, keep searching – there are way more areas of support now. There are many treatments and therapies available that can alleviate symptoms.

Every day, I work with women to help them understand their bodies, embrace the changes, and find their own paths to strength, balance, and joy. Everyone's menopause is somewhat different (individual) despite the many similarities – you are not weird; you are not losing the plot and you are very certainly not being taken over by aliens!

If you are reading this and are thinking to yourself, "I've tried many of these things before Jane and they simply haven't helped" then I encourage you to consider this: bringing about a difference, creating something more desirable is totally possible if you really want it and decide it's worth the effort, but often requires first, a change of belief. Limiting beliefs create our habits and habits keep us stuck. Change your belief and then change your habit. The author Mark Twain had an observation about how we can change unwanted ways of thinking and behaving "habit is coaxed downstairs a step at a time," in other words I see this as just trying one small thing – tiny changes all add up to making a big difference.

My story is one of resilience and reinvention, proving that even in the face of life's most challenging moments, there is always a way forward. Through sharing my journey (it's a brief rendition in this chapter), I aim to inspire others to not only survive but thrive during this significant phase of life. Embrace the opportunities your menopause years provide.

What I have learnt is to share with good friends, move forward with conviction, ask for what you want, explore new adventures, and embrace the new opportunities that this time of life may present. In other words – it's over to you now – with all my love x.

Jane's 3am Bread (Origin Unknown)

Ingredients:

550g Spelt flour
200g Wholemeal flour
100g Barley flour
a large pinch of salt
42g fresh yeast
530 mls warm water
1 teaspoon of olive oil for greasing

Method:

1. Preheat the oven to 200 C.
2. Grease the loaf tin, bottom, and sides with the olive oil.
3. In a large bowl mix the 3 flours together with the sea salt.
4. In another smaller bowl dissolve the yeast in the warm water.
5. Pour the yeast mixture into the flour and mix well.

6. Knead the dough with your hands until you get a smooth consistency (you can use a food processor with a dough hook – but where is the fun in that!)
7. Empty the dough into the greased loaf tin and lightly score the dough with a sharp knife.
8. Leave the dough to rise for 30 minutes until it has doubled in size.
9. Place the loaf in the center of the hot oven.
10. After 15 minutes turn the oven down to 160 C and bake for a further 45 minutes
11. Then enjoy.

Shamilla Williams-Haynes

Founder of Shamilla Speaks

https://www.linkedin.com/in/shamilla-williams-haynes-a2949911/
https://www.facebook.com/toplevelprogram/
https://shamillaspeaks.com/

Shamilla is a homemaker and grandmother residing in the beautiful island of Aruba. She has carved out a niche for herself as an influential professional speaker. Her multilingual skill allows her to communicate effectively in English, Spanish, Dutch, and Papiamento, making her an invaluable asset in diverse speaking engagements.

Her ability to coach your audience, -no matter the format- with practical examples is her secret sauce. She is an Expert who speaks; having "been there, done it," and is passionate about showing others to do it too. Authenticity and depth of knowledge make her a standout in the public speaking and coaching field.

The programs she has developed are:

- **The Period Power:** A comprehensive program designed to educate and empower women about their menstrual health.
- **"Let's Talk Menopause":** The often-overlooked and misunderstood aspects of menopause.

Shamilla's genuine approach has earned her respect and admiration from around the world.

Menopause is not a sickness it is the DESSERT life serves us

By Shamilla Williams-Haynes

A Milestone in My Journey

This evening was the culmination of a successful day. It will be my third speech for the day on International Women's Day 2023.

I was about to take the stage in a room filled with over 150 women who came together on this beautiful island of Aruba to celebrate womanhood. The prime minister of the island was on stage delivering her opening speech for the Leading Ladies Conference. I was to speak after her on the theme "Let's Talk Female Hormones & Real Life."

Oh. And what a stage… The ballroom of one of the hotels with an iconic view of the round-a-bout with flags of most of the countries we welcome tourists from, and the runway of the airplanes bringing those tourists to the island.

I was at the back of the room being mic'd up and without any notice just like cravings during pregnancy these PALPITATIONS hit me. The feeling is overwhelming; you think your heart will burst through your dress any moment and that every person in that room—even if you're facing their backs—can see you.

As a professional speaker, I know that the show must go on. So without any hesitation, I started running from one side of the room to the other and back about 3 times, this is a practical tip that helped me overcome my moments of palpitations and yes, of course, some people looked back and gave me the eye. As the master of ceremony called my name I took—in my mind—a sprint, which most likely was just a hasty walk, and took the stage. My entrance was invented right there and then but... I was calm and had that menopause symptom under control. I used what happened a couple of minutes ago as the icebreaker for my talk.

What Is Menopause?

A milestone, comparable to your first menstruation, or with any big life's celebration. It is on the day you accomplished exactly consecutive 12 months without having your period, Period.

Menopause is a biological process that every woman will experience if she lives long enough. It marks the end of menstruation and fertility, occurring typically between the ages of 45 and 55. Menopause, like any other major life transition, brings about significant changes. These changes can be challenging, but they also offer opportunities for growth and self-improvement. Embracing change means letting go of the past and looking forward to the future with optimism and an open mind.

Understanding Menopause: A Natural Transition

The transition to menopause, known as perimenopause, can begin several years before the last menstrual period and is characterized by changes in menstrual cycle patterns, hot flashes, night sweats, and other symptoms. While these physical changes are often discussed, the emotional and psychological aspects of menopause are equally important. Menopause is not a sickness; it is the dessert life serves us for being women; it's a rite of passage, a natural evolution in a woman's life that signifies maturity, wisdom, and resilience.

Resilience is the ability to bounce back from adversity, and menopause is an opportunity to cultivate and demonstrate this quality.

Wisdom, another gift of menopause, comes from years of life experience. It is the ability to make sound decisions, show empathy, and offer guidance to others. As we navigate menopause, we gain insights that can benefit not only ourselves but also those around us.

Sharing our wisdom with younger generations can help them prepare for their own journeys and foster a greater sense of community and support.

The physical and emotional challenges of menopause can test our limits, but they also reveal our strength and resilience. By facing these challenges head-on, we develop a deeper understanding of ourselves and our capabilities.

As you can read in the other chapters, initially, the symptoms of menopause are overwhelming. We call this the perimenopause stage. Your body will start producing fewer reproductive hormones; something that you're not accustomed to. Each of us will react differently to it. If you get the known hot flashes, mood swings, or heavy menstruation you will know very soon… aha, I'm getting there.

How Menopause Affected Me

If you're like me, then joint pain, knee instability, protein intolerance, high blood pressure, and eczema will dominate your life. They can appear in the morning and disappear within a day or two. These changes were more than just physical; they affected my self-esteem and my relationships. I felt like I was losing control over my body and emotions.

Not satisfied with the approach of several physicians, which was to only help me get rid of the pain, I started researching my symptoms and over some time I realized that all these symptoms always had a list the possibilities, and menopause was always mentioned in the list.

My journey

My journey through menopause was a journey of self-discovery. I realized that menopause was not something to be feared or dreaded but a natural part of life that offered new opportunities for personal growth and development. I began to appreciate the wisdom that comes with age and experience, and I embraced the resilience that menopause demanded. I learnt that Menopause is a milestone just like your first menstruation, first relationship, first... you name it.

Menopause Is a Date

This milestone—twelve consecutive months of absence of your menstrual period, often laden with societal stigma and personal apprehension, felt like a momentous celebration. Much like my first big promotion at work or my wedding day, it was a significant life event, one that signaled the beginning of a new chapter.

As time went on, I began to see menopause differently. Instead of viewing it as a series of unpleasant symptoms, I started to see it as a powerful transition—a time to reflect, grow, and reinvent—myself. This shift in perspective was not immediate; it was the result of a conscious effort and desire to embrace this new phase of life with grace and positivity.

One pivotal moment in my realization was during one of my long sleepless nights. As I lay in my bed, my husband turned to me and hugged me as his form of support during these episodes, I felt a deep sense of peace and acceptance wash over me. I understood that my body was changing, but these changes did not diminish my worth or my identity. Instead, they added to the tapestry of my life, making it richer and more complex.

Why I Share and Educate

I share my experience with menopause not only to destigmatize it but also to empower other women. There is a pervasive cultural narrative that views menopause as a decline or a loss. This narrative is not only incorrect but harmful. By sharing our stories and educating others, we can shift the narrative to one that celebrates menopause as a natural and empowering phase of life.

Education is the key to dispelling myths and promoting a positive attitude towards aging and menopause. When women are informed about what to expect during menopause and how to manage symptoms, they are better equipped to handle the transition with confidence and grace. Knowledge is power, and by educating ourselves and others, we can transform the experience of menopause from one of fear and uncertainty to one of empowerment and resilience.

Personal Tips for Navigating Menopause

- **Prioritize Self-Care:** Taking time for yourself is crucial during menopause. This can include activities like yoga, meditation, or simply enjoying a quiet moment with a good book. Self-care helps to manage stress and promotes overall well-being.

- **Stay Active:** Regular physical activity can help alleviate many of the symptoms of menopause. Exercise boosts mood, supports cardiovascular health, and helps maintain a healthy weight. Find an activity you enjoy, whether it's walking, swimming, or dancing, and make it a part of your routine.

- **Healthy Diet:** A balanced diet rich in fruits, vegetables, lean proteins, and whole grains can support overall health during menopause. Foods high in calcium and vitamin D are particularly important for bone health. Avoid excessive caffeine and alcohol, as they can exacerbate symptoms like hot flashes and sleep disturbances.

- **Seek Support:** Connecting with others who are going through the same experience can be incredibly comforting. Support groups, whether in person or online, offer a space to share experiences, seek advice, and find encouragement. Don't hesitate to reach out to friends, family, or healthcare professionals for support.

- **Educate Yourself:** Understanding what is happening to your body can help you feel more in control. Read books, attend workshops, or talk to your doctor about what to expect during menopause and how to manage symptoms.

A Funny Story with a Lesson

One evening, while attending a birthday dinner, I experienced one of the most intense hot flashes I'd ever had. The room felt like it was closing in on me, and I could feel the sweat starting to trickle down my back. In a desperate attempt to cool down, I discreetly pulled out a handheld fan from my purse and began fanning myself vigorously. The noise of the fan caught the attention of the people around me, and soon enough, everyone at the table was laughing. While initially mortifying, the incident turned into a hilarious story that I now share with friends and family. It taught me the importance of humor in dealing with life's challenges.

Empowerment through Education

Education empowers us to take control of our health and well-being. By understanding the physiological changes that occur during menopause, we can make informed decisions about our health. Being proactive about our health allows us to approach menopause with confidence and a sense of empowerment.

Breaking the Silence: The Importance of Open Dialogue

One of the most significant barriers to a positive menopause experience is the silence that often surrounds it. Many women feel ashamed or embarrassed to talk about their symptoms, fearing judgment or misunderstanding. This silence perpetuates the stigma and leaves women feeling isolated and unsupported.

Breaking the silence means having open and honest conversations about menopause. It means sharing our experiences, asking questions, and seeking support. By fostering an environment of open dialogue, we can create a culture that normalizes menopause and supports women through this transition.

The Role of Healthcare Providers

Healthcare providers play a crucial role in supporting women through menopause. It is essential to have a trusted healthcare provider who can offer guidance, support, and appropriate treatment options. Women should feel empowered to discuss their symptoms and concerns with their providers and to seek out information and resources that can help them navigate menopause.

The Power of Community

There is immense power in the community. Connecting with others who are experiencing or have experienced menopause can provide a sense of solidarity and support. Whether through support groups, online forums, or informal gatherings, sharing our stories and listening to others can make a significant difference in how we experience menopause.

Menopause often prompts a re-evaluation of identity. As we transition out of our reproductive years, we may question our roles, our purpose, and our sense of self. This period of introspection can be an opportunity to redefine ourselves and explore new interests, passions, and goals.

Creative Expression and Self-Discovery

Creative expression can be a powerful tool for self-discovery and healing during menopause. Whether through writing, painting, music, or other forms of artistic expression, engaging in creative activities can help us process our emotions, explore our identities, and find joy and fulfillment.

Spiritual Growth and Mindfulness

For many women, menopause is a time of spiritual growth and a deeper connection with themselves. Practices such as mindfulness, meditation, and yoga can support this inner journey, helping us to cultivate a sense of peace, acceptance, and gratitude.

Menopause and Relationships

Menopause can also impact our relationships with partners, family, and friends. Open communication and mutual support are key to navigating these changes together. Sharing our experiences with loved ones can foster understanding and strengthen our relationships.

Self-Compassion and Acceptance

One of the most important lessons of menopause is self-compassion. Being kind to ourselves, accepting our bodies and our experiences, and letting go of perfectionism are essential components of a positive menopause journey. Self-compassion allows us to embrace our imperfections and celebrate our strengths.

Humor: Finding Joy in the Journey

Humor is a powerful tool for coping with the challenges of menopause. Finding humor in our experiences can lighten the emotional load and bring joy to the journey. Sharing funny stories and moments with others can create a sense of connection and laughter, making the transition more enjoyable.

Summarizing the Journey

In this chapter, we've explored the journey of menopause, from the initial challenges to the realization of its empowering potential. Menopause is a natural transition that offers opportunities for growth, wisdom, and self-discovery. By embracing this phase of life with resilience and positivity, we can redefine menopause as a prize of womanhood, as the dessert life serves us.

Call to Action: Embrace, Educate, Empower

I invite you to join me in redefining menopause—share your story, educate others, and embrace this transformative phase with grace and positivity. Together, we can create a future where menopause is celebrated as a natural and empowering part of a woman's life journey. Let us break the silence, foster open dialogue, and support each other in this journey of resilience, wisdom, and life.

You can email at toplevelprogram@gmail.com for more information or to book a workshop on Menopause is not a sickness.

Shamilla Williams-Haynes.

Kylye

Cyclical Cultures
The Menopause Coordinator

https://www.linkedin.com/in/coachkylye
https://www.linktr.ee/coachkylye
www.cyclicalcultures.com

Kylye Ann Ralston is a Life Enthusiast, Storyteller, and Believer in Humanity. Her work centers on guiding women through the transformational power of menopause, helping them reclaim their inner wisdom and embrace their cyclical nature. Drawing from her own spiritual journey, Kylye empowers women to see menopause as a time of renewal and reconnection with their true selves. Through her teachings, she helps others break free from societal conditioning and embrace this life phase with reverence. While her journey into the corporate world is new, Kylye is passionate about creating cyclical cultures within workplaces, fostering environments that honor the menopause transition and support women's emotional and spiritual well-being. Kylye believes that by redefining menopause, women can shape their legacy and leave an impact for generations to come.

Happily Ever Menopause

By Kylye Ralston

If your womb space were a storybook, what kind of tale would it tell? Characters, plot, foreshadowing, and endings. What sort of narrative would your womb weave?

After years of societally conditioning women to deny and resent the womb as the sacred space of creation that it truly is, it is now time to awaken our power and rewrite the narrative.

A woman's womb is a space of creation—not just for creating humans but for creativity expressed through her roles, her career, her children, her art, her ideas, and her impact. Each woman is the creator—the creatrix! The power lies within. It is time to recognize and honor this creation space. It is time to tell the story of the womb.

The divide in our world goes beyond politics or personal preferences; it's a deep separation from our true selves. Women have been conditioned to hate their wombs, using this sacred space without gratitude and sometimes with disgust. This starts at menstruation and continues through their lives. Many women feel ashamed of their cycles, trying to ignore them rather than embracing them as part of a natural rhythm. Even after childbirth, there's often no appreciation for their bodies' incredible work, only demands and blame.

Menopause represents a crucial moment for women to reconnect with their bodies. Perimenopause is a call to stop mistreating ourselves and to start valuing our bodies as our soul mates, the vessels we chose for this life. Redefining menopause is essential.

Let's embark on a journey to explore the new and redefined narrative of your menopausal transition. Humans are meaning-making creatures, and how women understand their lives matters deeply. Just as computers need updates to function well, we also need to refresh our perspective on menopause. This is the moment to shift the script and embrace a new understanding of this phase of life.

Every great story has plot twists, hurdles, and moments of deep struggle that you must overcome before reaching the grand finale. Without these elements, the story would lack excitement, purpose, and a satisfying climax. Imagine your life as a storybook. What kind of story is it? Are you the main character? What do you want it to be filled with? How do you want it to end? Would others enjoy reading this novel?

Remember, this story is a choose-your-own-ending adventure. You are the author, narrator, and protagonist. You get to decide. Each day, each moment, each thought is a choice. Even choosing not to pick up the pen is a choice.

Once upon a time, you grew up with fairytales—stories steeped in societal expectations. These tales promised that you would fall in love, get married, and live happily ever after. Recently, the script has changed. Now, it suggests that you must find yourself, become a hero, fall in love, get married, be an attentive partner, manage a career, contribute to the community, care for children, and do it all with makeup, stylish clothes, and a smile.

While this new narrative might seem liberating, it means you have to juggle even more responsibilities. You are now tasked with everything a whole community once shared. And still, the story concludes with "happily ever after." But what comes next?

Happily Ever…Menopause?

Wait… Cut! No one prepared us for this chapter.

To understand this, we must journey back—way back—to a time when a woman's power was revered and storytelling held deep significance. Are you ready?

There was a time when a woman's power was honored—a time before the modern-day fairytale—when storytelling was the primary means of passing down information.

Many moons ago, women and men walked beside each other as equals. They were human beings with different strengths and weaknesses, balancing each other and creating harmony.

Masculinity provided a container and a safe space for femininity to create and flow. Like all things in nature, there was a natural ease and balance in this divine relationship.

Women's lives were easily marked into three clear phases:

Maiden, Mother, and Matriarch. Each phase held its own beauty and value.

The Maiden was full of curiosity and wonder. She expressed herself freely, losing hours in the things she loved to do. She embodied innocence and joy. She did not hold back her emotions but explored them without judgment and made play sacred.

A Maiden entered her Mother years when the first rite of passage presented itself: Menarche, the start of her moon time. This was celebrated and honored. The internal cauldron of creativity within her was activated. She had become cyclical. She joined the sun, stars, moon, seasons, and the tides. She now carried within her all four seasons of Mother Earth, cyclically existing within her every month. She was connected to nature and tapped into the power of being able to do a multitude of things at once! All women are in the creation phase here. The womb is a creative space. Some would bear children, others not. The mother phase is more than creating human life; it is about creating life—be it art, love, relationships, purpose, or career. It's about nurturing and bringing meaningful projects to life. All she learned in the years of play and wonder turned into new projects with deeper meaning. This phase is characterized by nurturing others and creating many things in the world. A woman in the Mother phase bled each month from the portal of life between her legs, as predictably as the sun and moon. If the bleeding stopped, she would begin to grow in her belly area, and after nine months of nurturing the elixir of life, a new life would be brought into the world! Once again, she would return to her cyclical bleeding.

The final phase—from Mother to Matriarch—is marked by the second rite of passage: Menopause, the cessation of moon time. Suddenly, all the energy that was once expended each month through bleeding is retained within her. Imagine the wonder and perhaps confusion when this change was first observed. As months passed with no menstrual blood, curiosity would have been piqued, wondering if this energy was being conserved for a new creation, but no child appeared.

Now, her moon times are complete. She holds the elixir of life within her, having undergone a profound transformation. The energy that was once spent each month—mentally, spiritually, and physically—is now hers to harness. She has become a keeper of wisdom, having journeyed through all her moon times, and this phase is her opportunity to channel that accumulated energy into new endeavors, insights, and contributions.

She learned during her Mother's years how to nurture others, including people, projects, and things. Now, she must apply that same nurturing herself. Women who lived this long were seen as elders, wise women, and wisdom keepers. They played a crucial role in passing down knowledge essential for the well-being of the species.

These women were now confident and comfortable in their sexuality, engaging in powerful and nurturing roles such as delivering babies (e.g., midwives), creating remedies (e.g., herbalists), and being philosophical thinkers who defied the norm and advanced human evolution. They carried multiple generations of wisdom and worked alongside masculine elders to create harmony.

Then, one day, a thought emerged—one that would alter the course of history. A man, deeply hurt and unable to win the love of the woman he sought, decided to disrupt the inherent balance of our natural world. This story is woven into many narratives, such as the ancient Grail legends and the tale of the well-maidens. Perhaps it was influenced by accusations of heresy tied to emerging Christianity. Or maybe it was the action of one persuasive individual threatened by the power women held, who sought to crush that power. The balance was disrupted.

And so began the journey that would lead up to a world wide trauma known as the witch hunts. People have long wondered why this disruption occurred, but does the reason truly matter? What is more intriguing is why this power imbalance remains shrouded in silence. For over three centuries, people were hunted—primarily those who stood firmly in their power. Approximately eighty percent of those convicted in these witch hunts were women, most of whom were over forty, likely navigating their menopausal transition.

These women, who had once held a revered position of wisdom and power, became targets in a tragic quest to reclaim control and suppress the feminine power that had once been celebrated. The witch hunts were not merely a historical anomaly but a reflection of a deeper fear and resistance to the powerful transformation that menopause represents—a transition from external validation to inner strength and wisdom.

We begin with the witch hunts because their impact continues to resonate with us today. The women who lived through these times endured trauma that would echo through the centuries. To witness a person being burned alive in a town square was an unfathomable experience. To smell the flesh and hear the cries of the condemned and their loved ones created a profound fear that was passed down through generations.

Women became terrified to embrace their own power. They feared speaking up or doing anything that could be perceived as magical.

These women were powerful individuals, not witches.

The next generation inherited this fear and carried forward the legacy of suppressed wisdom. The knowledge and power of women, along with the trauma they experienced, were passed down to their children.

If one had lived during this period, they would have instructed their children to hide their power for their own safety. Mothers confessed to being witches to save their daughters, leaving one to face death while the other struggled with survivor's guilt. This was not merely a time of men hunting women but also women turning against each other. A deliberate wedge was driven between people, intended to prevent women from stepping into their power and enforce conformity.

This divide lasted for approximately 300 years. While we discuss other major historical events that caused widespread trauma, the global gendercide of the witch hunts is often overlooked. It has been around 300 years since the witch hunts officially ended, though it's worth noting that similar persecutions still occur in some parts of the world. This period marked the end of an era when women were once held as sacred.

Women became viewed as resources with specific tasks, losing agency over their bodies. Fast forward to today.

Baby Boomers, having experienced menopause, now reflect on their lives, wondering if they missed something. Generation X, following closely behind, is the first generation to be prominently featured in the limelight of social media. This generation, known for its hyper-independence and willingness to address taboo topics, is sparking the conversation about menopause.

Millennials, with their fresh perspectives and compassionate hearts, are bringing new ideas and advocating for inclusivity. Their ideologies are reshaping how we work and perceive transitions.

All three generations are either affected or about to be affected by the menopausal transition.

There is a collective curiosity about our identity and purpose. A renewed inspiration is emerging to find meaning in our lives. The fight against patriarchy is more vigorous than ever before. More women in the workforce are experiencing menopause than at any other time in history.

As humans born with a womb standing in today's age, we find ourselves at a crossroads. We can choose to become bitter and withdrawn, fading into the background as society has conditioned us to believe we should.

In this narrative, we may silently grow old after a lifetime of caring for others, walking the tightrope of equanimity—never too much, never enough. This choice, driven by exhaustion, is certainly valid.

Alternatively, we can view this natural phase of life as an opportunity to embrace our power as the main character in our own story. We can approach menopause with intention, emerging from it with a powerful voice that will impact the upcoming future generations. By making this choice, we also heal the generations before us, breaking free from the trauma passed down from women who endured widespread persecution and more.

We now have the space to remember that we are cyclical beings and that the creative force within us extends beyond reproduction. We have earned the right to step into our most authentic selves. We are healing the rift between women, supporting and uplifting each other. We are rediscovering the trust and importance of the connection that once bound us together.

It all starts with a thought.

You get to choose that thought.

You get to decide how you will redefine menopause.

You are not only the main character in this story; you are the narrator and the author. You hold the pen.

To confront this choice, you must face the portal of decision.

The one thing that allows you to see yourself—the magic mirror. Yes, just like in the fairytales. In those stories, the patriarchy portrayed the mirror as evil, and it has likely seemed malevolent in your life as well, casting societal spells of expectation upon you and convincing you that you are defined by your appearance.

Each woman will encounter the magic of the mirror on the wall. Some may already be consumed by its dark forces, allowing it to dictate the course of their story. For those who choose to be better and bold, who are courageous enough to confront the mirror and resist its dark magic, this is your ultimate test.

To unlock the true magic of the mirror, you must stand naked before it. Yes, naked. This is your body, not your enemy. Allow yourself to confront all the dark thoughts that have accompanied every glance in the mirror. Yet, we must listen to these inner voices. Don't push them away, and please don't ignore them. Feel them deeply within your body.

Acknowledge all the wounds you've internalized, like a spell cast upon yourself. Recognize the beliefs that seeped in over time, starting from a comment or circumstance and slowly becoming a poison. Recall all the negative things said about your body and how you've repeated those words to yourself.

Once you've processed these feelings, take a step closer to the magic mirror. Reflect on how many of these thoughts were about your appearance. How many were sexualized? Is this all you are?

Even menopause has been reduced to what some doctors call "bikini medicine"—focused solely on breasts and reproductive organs. But menopause is so much more than that. It affects our brains and our emotions and is a profound spiritual journey. It is not merely about our sexual organs or our ability to reproduce. Nor whether we still bleed or not.

So, gaze into the mirror and remember all the things your body has done for you. Dive deep into this reflection. This is where we begin to truly redefine menopause, where we start to lift the spell that the mirror has cast upon us.

Examine each of your scars. Reflect on how often your body has endured pain, injuries, and even abuse. Consider how many times you have mistreated it. Acknowledge how long your body has been with you, showing up day after day.

Try to grasp the absolute magnificence of this intricate machine. How much pleasure has your body provided you? Think of the joy derived from food, the pleasure of scents, the music that has moved you, the words from loved ones, the sights you've witnessed, the textures you've felt, the warmth of hugs, the sweetness of kisses, and the ecstasy of orgasms.

When you look at your head, which houses your brain, express gratitude for the safety it has provided for that incredible supercomputer of yours. Reflect on all you have accomplished and experienced because of your remarkable brain.

PLAY! Consider how much play your body has enabled—riding bikes, painting, exploring, playing games, and tossing rocks into a lake.

At this moment, it is crucial to partner with our bodies. This partnership begins with our minds deciding that it can happen. Our bodies have stored countless moments we brushed aside for the sake of harmony. They have endured toxins and likely intentional poisons we've introduced. They have been beaten down mentally and emotionally by our own thoughts, often every time we glanced in the mirror.

No more. Our bodies are our ONE vehicle in this life, and we have intentionally been trained to hate them unless they are perfect.

Now place your hand on your womb space. Even if your womb is no longer physically present, this space remains significant. It deserves its own moment in this spell-breaking process.

Reflect on when you first began to harbor negative feelings about your womb. Was it when you reached womanhood at menarche? When a boy mocked you for having your period? Or when your mother conveyed that your period was something to be ashamed of and taught you to hide it?

Remember these moments.

When you were in the Maiden phase, you cherished your womb. You played with dolls, looked up to women, and dreamed of becoming a mother someday. You would place your hand on your tummy or someone else's and speak of babies with excitement.

So, when did you start to harbor negative feelings toward your womb? This part of the spell-breaking exercise is about revisiting the negative energy you've directed at this space. Recall the things you've said about it and the negative emotions you've associated with it. Did you create life from this space without ever pausing to offer gratitude or marvel at the sheer magic of how it all works?

This is NOT your fault. The sacredness was lost during the witch hunts, and the true spells were cast upon us during that time. But here we are now, breaking those spells.

This is the moment to show gratitude for this space. Many women do not honor or appreciate their menstrual cycles—this lack of reverence is something we've been taught. But we have changed that now. Here we rewrite the story, shifting from his story to her story.

Please close your eyes for a moment and feel the immense energy our bodies expend each month to bleed. Really connect with this sensation.

As women, we know that this process demands an extraordinary amount of energy from every part of our bodies, as it involves the preparation and release of the potential for creating human life. This energy, which has contributed to populating the planet, resides within us each month—until menopause.

Enter menopause...

No longer do we expend that energy monthly; instead, we harness and use it. We retain the elixir of life, holding within us this incredible reservoir of creative energy for the rest of our time here. This is our earned wisdom.

Can you feel the power of that?

The patriarchy sensed it, too, 600 years ago. And so, they hunted us.

With proper unlearning and women choosing to genuinely partner with their bodies, we will fully step into the most powerful phase of our lives: The Final Act.

The final act is always the best part of the story, wouldn't you agree?

Your assignment is still ongoing. Step closer to the mirror.

Sit cross-legged in front of it. We now need to stare into our own eyes.

She is there—the wise woman within. She holds all the chapters of you that have ever been written. You catch glimpses of her from time to time, perhaps in a streak of silver hair. She is there, patiently waiting.

The spell of the magic mirror has kept you from her until now.

Ask her to step forward. She is not just your body or your mind; she is your spirit, your soul. She carries your bloodline forward from two families—the essence that will be remembered or even passed on after you are gone. She holds both your pain and your purpose.

Inside these eyes, remember each chapter of yourself. The you in the womb, the you in the delivery room, the young toddler you, the school-age you, the pubescent you, the young lady, the woman—all the characters you have played out up to now.

This exercise may need to be repeated. It may be painful to confront. The mirror's magic is strong, and facing it will require courage and time. There is much to undo. As you sit here facing yourself, remember to have self-compassion.

This is the magic that will reverse the mirror's spell. You have practiced self-compassion throughout your life with others; now it's time to apply that practice to yourself. Treat yourself as you would treat someone you deeply care about.

Speak to the child version of yourself as you would to a young child. Console the teenage version; you would be a friend going through their own struggles. Offer the adult version of yourself the understanding and support you would extend to a dear friend.

Ask each version of yourself what they needed in those moments and then offer them what they ask for.

Take your time. This spell has been with you for many years, and breaking it will require great courage and effort.

I send you love and light as you work to reverse the mirror's dark magic and return to the natural flow and power of the universe to which you belong.

Find my free meditation here to walk you through
the exercise we just explored:
linktr.ee/coachkylye

The menopausal transition is the grand adventure of your story. This is the third act, where you get to decide what type of story you are in. Is it a fairytale? A comedy? A thriller? It is, in fact, a choose-your-own-adventure. YOU decide.

It will be challenging, but now you know the secret: to partner with your body and undo what has been done. This is how you live fully "happily ever after."

You shift the script and step into the unspoken phase of life, embracing menopause on purpose. After all, you could spend up to 40% of your life in this phase. That's an incredible amount of time to leave a legacy for the next seven generations.

The world needs your wisdom.

Thank you for choosing to embrace this journey and break the spell.

Thank you for sharing your intergenerational wisdom with the world instead of continuing to conform to the societal divide that keeps us apart from each other and from ourselves.

Now that you are stepping into your choose-your-own-adventure YOUR way, other women will look up to. You've taken control of your narrative—embracing your unique beauty, redefining menopause, and creating a life beyond the conventional "Happily Ever After."

This is not **THE END**.

Kylye Ann Ralston
Life Enthusiast. Story Teller. Believer in Humanity.

Dr. Marva Williams

Founder of Shhh... Menopause Wellness

https://www.linkedin.com/in/marva-williams/
https://www.facebook.com/profile.php?id=100075831986982
https://www.instagram.com/shhhh.menopausewellness
https://shhhmenopausewellness.com/

Dr. Marva Williams (Hons), is the founder of Shhh... Menopause Wellness, a Menopause Coach, and a Counsellor. She specialises in creating natural symptom led menopause solutions and educating women on the benefits of clean ingredients. Through Shhh..., her mission is to enhance women's wellness, break the silence around menopause, and foster community growth. She has dedicated herself to creating holistic, botanical formulations. Her work became even more personal after surviving a near-death experience in 2019 due to undiagnosed perimenopausal symptoms. This led her to develop products specifically designed to support women during perimenopause and postmenopause. Marva also develops skincare solutions for eczema, burns, and patients undergoing chemotherapy or radiotherapy, training medical professionals and practioners in holistic approaches using botanical solutions that deliver fast, effective results.

Surviving Menopause: My Journey from Near-Death to Business Owner and Menopause Coach

By Dr. Marva Williams

In 2019, my life was a whirlwind of non-stop work. As a dedicated professional, I was constantly juggling multiple responsibilities, from meeting tight deadlines to managing complex projects. Each day was a marathon, starting early and ending late, often blurring the lines between weekdays and weekends.

I pushed through every day, even when I didn't feel well. There were countless mornings when I woke up feeling exhausted, my body pleading for rest. But I ignored the signs, driven by an unyielding commitment to my responsibilities. My work ethic was built on the belief that hard work and perseverance were the keys to success, and I was determined to live up to that standard.

There were days when fatigue and discomfort threatened to overwhelm me. My body ached, my energy levels were depleted, and I experienced bouts of dizziness and headaches. Yet, I soldiered on, convincing myself that I just needed to push through a little longer and that 'rest' could wait. I had always prided myself on my resilience and ability to handle stress, so slowing down wasn't an option I considered. Unbeknownst to me, a storm was brewing within my body.

The symptoms I dismissed as minor inconveniences were actually warnings of a more significant underlying issue. I was unaware of the hormonal changes taking place, changes that would soon bring my relentless grind to an abrupt and terrifying halt.

Looking back, I realize how deeply ingrained the culture of overwork was in my life. The relentless pursuit of achievement and the constant pressure to perform had become second nature to me. I neglected my health and well-being, prioritizing my career above all else. This unsustainable lifestyle was about to catch up with me in the most alarming way possible, forcing me to confront the consequences of my relentless grind.

The breaking point came suddenly and without warning. It was an ordinary day, one like many others, filled with tasks and responsibilities. My mother asked me to collect a prescription for her from the doctor's surgery. Little did I know this would mark a turning point in my life.

As I stood waiting for my turn to speak to the receptionist, I felt a wave of dizziness wash over me. My vision blurred, and a cold sweat broke out on my forehead. I tried to steady myself, taking deep breaths and willing the sensation to pass. But instead of abating, the dizziness intensified. The room began to spin, the walls closing in on me, and I knew something was terribly wrong.

My legs buckled beneath me. I collapsed to the floor, the world around me fading into a swirl of shadows and muffled sounds. Panic surged through me as I realized I had no control over my body. The voices of those around me seemed distant, almost as if they were underwater. I could faintly hear the urgency and concern in their tones, but I couldn't respond.

Darkness closed in, enveloping me in an abyss of fear and helplessness. My last conscious thought was a desperate plea for God to help me. When I came to, I was disoriented and confused. The harsh fluorescent lights above me made my head throb, and I blinked, trying to make sense of my surroundings.

Doctors surrounded me, and I remember a voice saying, "She's back!" Their faces were a mix of relief and concentration. They had just resuscitated me, bringing me back from the brink. The gravity of the situation slowly dawned on me, and a chill of terror ran down my spine.

I had come frighteningly close to death, and the experience shook me to my core.

One of the doctors leaned over me, his expression grave yet reassuring. "You gave us quite a scare," he said gently. "But you're going to be alright. We're going to take good care of you. An ambulance is on its way."

As I lay there, still trying to process what had happened, the reality of my situation hit me like a tidal wave. My relentless pace and refusal to acknowledge the warning signs my body was sending had led me to this point. The collapse was not just a physical breakdown; it was a stark reminder of the fragility of life and the dire consequences of ignoring one's health.

The terror of that moment stayed with me long after I left the hospital. It was a wake-up call, a harsh lesson that forced me to reevaluate my life and priorities. The collapse was the beginning of a journey, one that would lead me to a deeper understanding of my body and the urgent need to care for it. It was a terrifying experience, one that shook me to my core and set the stage for profound transformation.

The ambulance arrived and took me to the hospital. As they began trying to draw blood, I felt like a pin cushion—my veins were difficult to find. When the results came back, I was in for a surprise: my haemoglobin, iron, and magnesium levels were alarmingly low.

They put me on intravenous drips and kept me in for a few days, running additional tests. After a few days, my levels had improved enough for them to release me, with a prescription for iron and magnesium tablets and instructions to see my doctor in a week.

You might have thought this was the end of my journey, but, in reality, it was only the beginning of a much longer and more challenging path. Two months later, I woke up one morning and realized I couldn't get out of bed. The sensation was strange and terrifying—something as simple as moving my legs, a task I had always taken for granted, now felt impossible. I tried again and again, willing my legs to respond, but they remained stubbornly motionless. A surge of panic welled up inside me as the terrifying realization dawned: "I might be paralyzed!" My mind raced with fear and confusion, desperately trying to make sense of this sudden loss of mobility and what it might mean for my future.

Little did I know, this moment marked the beginning of a journey that would eventually lead to the creation of Shhh… Menopause Wellness— a company dedicated to supporting peri- and post-menopausal women.

In my panic, I reached for my phone and called my little sister, Maylene. She rushed to my room, her voice full of urgency. "Marva, get up! Stop messing around and get up!" But I could only respond, "I can't." Sensing something was seriously wrong, she called out to our mom. When she arrived, I saw the confusion in their eyes slowly give way to a deeper understanding as the gravity of the situation began to sink in.

To this day, I have no idea how they managed to get me down two flights of stairs, but somehow, they did. They gave me a bed bath and immediately called an ambulance. When the paramedics arrived, every attempt to move me onto the stretcher was excruciating. My body felt like it was on fire, and I cried out in pain each time they touched me. Eventually, they administered an injection to numb the pain, which allowed them to lift me into the ambulance.

At the hospital, they took my blood for testing. When the results came back, I was even more confused. My haemoglobin and iron levels were dangerously low, and as the doctor explained, my magnesium levels were almost non-existent. The doctors were baffled, and I argued that it was impossible—I had been diligently taking the supplements prescribed to me months ago. The lack of magnesium in my body had caused my joints to seize up.

The doctors put me on intravenous drips and continued running various tests, but my condition remained a mystery. After a few days, a consultant came to see me. He asked numerous questions about my family history, and I struggled to provide answers. Fortunately, my mom was able to fill in the gaps. The professor suggested that I might be peri-menopausal and explained that my dairy and wheat intolerances, which I was aware of, were preventing me from absorbing enough nutrients despite the supplements.

To make matters worse, I also had fibroids, and the consultant suspected I was peri-menopausal. It was my first time hearing that term, so I asked what it meant. He simply told me that it meant my periods would eventually stop, and he offered no further explanation.

I was prescribed a cocktail of medications—morphine, Tramadol, Buscopan, along with ibuprofen and paracetamol. But after a week in the hospital, I still couldn't walk, so they sent me home with this mix of drugs.

My mom set up a bed for me in the living room. She and my sister had to help me shower and use the restroom. I felt utterly defeated and depressed, terrified that I might never walk again. I cried myself to sleep most nights, praying for a miracle.

Pastor Joshua from my church visited often, praying with me and bringing communion. But I was so frustrated. My mind felt foggy as if it were filled with cotton wool. After a few days, I decided I had enough. I decided to stop taking the medications and started doing some research. As my mind began to clear, I found the focus and determination to take control of my situation.

During my research, I discovered the potential benefits of transdermal magnesium—the process of absorbing magnesium through the skin. I realized that this method could effectively deliver magnesium directly into my body, bypassing the digestive system where I had absorption issues. With this in mind, I began experimenting by purchasing ingredients and creating my own magnesium mixtures. I also incorporated essential oils known for their anti-inflammatory properties.

As I began applying these transdermal magnesium solutions, I noticed a gradual improvement in my condition. Slowly but surely, I started to regain control over the pain that had once dominated my life. Remarkably, my legs began to regain movement, and by October, I could walk again. Not only did this approach help with my mobility, but I also found that my painful PMS symptoms significantly subsided while using transdermal magnesium.

I felt isolated and alone as I delved into extensive research on peri-menopause, trying to understand what it meant for me. I began exploring the symptoms and experimenting with natural remedies to manage them. The more I talked with friends and family, the more stories I heard from other women going through similar experiences. I created botanical solutions to address their symptoms because I realized there was a real need for new products that offered relief from menopause.

In early 2021, I made up my mind to start my business and launch a range of natural self-care and well-being products to help women experiencing peri-menopause and menopause. By November 2021, Shhh… Menopause Wellness was officially launched. I was determined to support as many women as possible, especially since so many had unanswered questions about how menopause affects their bodies.

In 2022, I embarked on a transformative journey to become a menopause coach and counselor. This decision was driven by my desire to expand my expertise and provide more comprehensive support to women navigating the challenging stages of menopause. Through this training, I gained a deeper understanding of the physical, emotional, and psychological aspects of menopause, enabling me to offer personalized guidance and effective solutions.

Since then, the impact of my work has been profound. I've developed a range of products that have significantly improved the lives of many women. For instance, Sleep Sound H20 has become a trusted companion for those struggling with insomnia and restless legs, with countless women expressing their gratitude for finally experiencing peaceful, restorative sleep. The Relieve and Ease Magnesium Mist has become a daily essential for many, offering much-needed relief from joint pain and muscle aches—a common issue during menopause.

One of the standout products in my range is Menocare Isoflavone Plus, a supplement that has become a go-to for women during both peri- and post-menopause. It's been particularly effective in helping manage symptoms like hot flashes, mood swings, and hormonal imbalances, allowing women to regain control over their bodies and lives during this transitional phase.

This journey of supporting women through menopause has been deeply fulfilling, and I've never looked back. Seeing the positive changes in the lives of those who use my products and hearing their stories of improved well-being is a constant reminder of why I chose this path. It has reinforced my commitment to continue developing innovative solutions and providing the best possible support for women during this crucial stage of life.

Tanya Kravcenko

Chartered Accountant & Author

https://www.linkedin.com/company/tanyakravcenko/
https://www.facebook.com/TheJellybeanTheory
https://www.instagram.com/tanyakravcenkonz/
www.tanyakravcenko.com

Tanya Kravcenko is a chartered accountant with a passion for financial literacy and has more than 20 years of industry experience. After spending her career supporting small businesses and entrepreneurs, Tanya noticed a significant gap in financial literacy among younger (and even older) generations. This inspired her to develop coaching sessions to empower people with the tools to make positive life choices and reach their full potential.

Navigating the Waves: Embracing Menopause as a Journey of Rediscovery

By Tanya Kravcenko

Menopause is one of those times in your life when you feel like you are going crazy! Some days you can cook a roast dinner and some days you look at all the vegetables you have prepared and the chicken and try to think how I can cook all this food so that it is ready to be eaten at the same time. It got worse if I had a glass of wine while I was cooking. I would start to think I did not have enough food so I would make a lot more. Sometimes, I would just give up and walk out of the kitchen and let the men finish the meal. Poor guys have no idea what is going on and we cannot explain our mindset to them either.

Once I learnt to just go with the flow and laugh at myself, life became easier. My partner knew that some days he may be asked to finish cooking the roast dinner and I could focus on one thing – drinking my glass of wine. My multitasking gifts had flown out the door.

I was in my 50s and running an accounting practice with 140 clients, a 7-acre hobby farm, solo mum to my daughter, and going through a separation from my ex. The stress accumulated during COVID times and when I got COVID brain fog kicked in and there was no way I could collate my client's financial statements for four months. My creative side of the brain became active and I was able to write easily. This is when my writing career started to take a turn and once, I completed the book *Charlie the Cyclist* I knew I wanted to teach financial literacy and mindset to young people. Teaching (advising) my clients was not easy as they had developed a negative mindset towards money and fear was making the decisions for them. When you work with young people they have not experienced many negative life experiences so they are open to trying new things.

The lucky thing for me during menopause was I did not lose my zest for sex – if anything, it went the opposite. My mum thought I needed to see a doctor about it and when I asked her if I should be worried, her advice was that I needed to buy a vibrator. Luckily enough, I had a new active partner who could keep up with my pace.

Body changes were huge! Suddenly, I developed breasts and put on weight in places I never knew were possible. As a fit and active person earlier, it was easy to keep the weight off but when I got long COVID, I was unable to breathe properly in order to run. So, my life became quite sedentary. Thankfully, I found a naturopath who understood menopause and the importance of gut health. With her suggestions, I slowly got rid of the brain fog and got back my zest for life after my relationship property settlement and saying goodbye to my mother.

Menopause and stress are not a good combination. The hormones that help stress management are reduced when you are going through menopause. As I was in fight-flight mode a lot during my relationship and afterwards when we were going through the relationship property settlement, I had to look at ways of reducing the things that were adding to my stress levels. I adapted a routine where I would write in a journal every morning for 5 minutes minimum about whatever was troubling me or what I was grateful for and what I wanted my life to look like. It was amazing what answers would come while I was writing and getting the negative thoughts out of my head helped too. I also would meditate during the day for half an hour and focus on deep breathing at the same time. I have three dogs and I am an active relaxant so I enjoy taking them for walks, focusing on breathing and looking at the scenery at the same time. This is called an active meditation. The work I did to bring my mindset into the present assisted with the reduction of my anxiety. I also changed my eating habits so that I was eating more plant-based food. Every week I would get a box of organic fruit and vegetables delivered and would make up meals from what was in the box. I never knew what was going to be delivered but it was always produce that was in season.

I think the word, menopause, has the word pause in it for a reason. Not only because our monthly cycle is on pause but it is a time in life when we need to slow down a bit and do the things in life that we enjoy the most. I had a boat and that was my best activity to fill my cup. It was a place where I could be in the ocean away from the hustle and bustle and I also liked fishing, so it was great to bring home some fish for dinner. It was the only place I could switch off from my business and role as a mother and I would get to enjoy the company of my friends too.

Menopause is a time to reflect and connect with our inner wisdom. I had two marriages and a long-term relationship and I knew what made me happy. I had spent 40 years trying to make other people happy and realised I had to love myself first. Doing acts of kindness for other people was what I had done my whole life from being the oldest daughter in a family of 5 children. My daughter is now nearly 18 so she is a young woman and just before my mother passed she complimented me on how I had done a great job teaching her how to be a strong independent woman. I learnt this from my mother and it is important to help fellow females as we transition through life. Menopause, marriage, motherhood, and career are a lot to juggle. But I am grateful I was able to show my daughter you can have it all if you put your mind to it and look after yourself first.

I was an older Mum and when I was going through menopause, my daughter was experiencing menstruation. It could be a very vocal situation for both of us sometimes when our anxiety levels got high but thankfully a good friend of mine taught me how to parent from love not fear. This helped our relationship a lot and I learnt to trust my daughter as she was discovering life as a 14-year-old in the COVID pandemic.

Menopause is different for everyone. The lucky ones just sail through and some people have a terrible time. I started my journey when I was 45 when my decision-making function wasn't as quick and I could not eat everything I desired as I used to. They are similar to symptoms of stress, so the doctors would recommend I take anxiety or depression medication. I found these took away the intensity of the symptoms but I still just did not feel right. I joined a Menopause Support group page and that is where I found I was not the only one struggling to understand the changes. It was great to be in a community and feel like what was happening to me was quite common and I was not going mad. It was also interesting to learn how dependent everyone was on HRT. The admin of the Facebook page would recommend everyone to increase their dose if they were still struggling with the symptoms. My naturopath joined the group but she was eventually blocked as the admin did not appreciate her natural solutions. I had heard bad things about HRT so was resistant to take it at first. My doctor was not that keen on prescribing it to me also. But finally, she gave me a prescription and within the first week I was sleeping better and the night sweats disappeared. I could taste food again and my anxiety reduced. The bad body odour disappeared too. But I still did not feel that energy where you wake up feeling fresh and ready for a new day.

I wanted to be on HRT for a short while so I made it my goal to be off it by the end of the year – that was for 6 months. In that time I restructured my life so that I was doing more things for myself. After being with a bipolar partner and then going through the nasty separation for another 8 years, I was emotionally drained. Thankfully, my doctor offered the free service of two ladies to visit me every week and do whatever I felt like doing. The first time we just sat and had a cup of tea. They were beautiful island ladies who had a great sense of humour. They totally understood how sometimes looking at a basket of washing that needed to be folded was overwhelming. The next week they went for a walk with me and my dogs. The following week, I asked them to help me move my boxes in my garage so I could park my car. I was so happy I could park my car in the garage. It was simple things like this that made a difference in my life but did not put too much pressure on myself. After 6 weeks, my self-motivation improved dramatically. I was able to get out of bed with energy every day, got my sense of humour back, enjoyed cooking again, and stopped cooking chicken tenders in the air fryer every night. I did not want to burden my family or friends with my symptoms and felt like I was failing at not being able to do everything like I used to. Being a high achiever and perfectionist it was hard to let go but once I stopped controlling what was happening with the changes in my body and mind and became accepting of who I was, life became simpler.

From being a member of the Facebook page, I got quite upset about how relationships were affected by menopause. Some women were being threatened by their partners to improve their weight or intimacy or they would leave. Some men were being treated with disrespect as the woman's patience was less and as they were tired more was expected of the men. The more I spoke to men about it, the more they wanted to understand our change of life. Therefore, I think it is important that we educate our men more. At school, young boys are told about what happens when a girl goes through puberty. We need a place for our men to have this information shared about menopause.

There were very few of us on the Facebook page who were looking for natural alternatives. So every day, I would reply to people's comments and suggest gut health, breathing exercises, meditation, walking, or any exercise. Over time other people would start to add health alternatives.

We need to go back to basics and release some of the stress. Women today have so many hats to wear compared to our mothers. Also, our food options are different from when my mother was going through menopause. What we put in our bodies via food and our minds has a huge impact on our energy levels. When we reduce the external noise and put more wholesome natural food into our bodies the ability to move and clarity for thinking changes dramatically.

My daughter adopted the same exercise and eating habits as me and she is also better off for it. The best thing we as women can do is support each other and show others how life can be made simple and you can enjoy a life of freedom if you really want to.

People blame the economy for their way of life but we all have choices. I was living in a very expensive house and could have got myself into debt to keep the same lifestyle when I separated from my partner but I chose Financial Freedom. It also gave me the opportunity to choose the career path I am now on and have the time to do what I want.

Menopause is a time to ask yourself what you want out of life and how you can be of service to others. The knowledge I have gained from being a Chartered Accountant set me up to teach financial literacy. When my daughter was young, I wanted to open up a school that had a similar format to Playcentre where learning was based on the child's interest. Little did I know that I was opening up a school that would be for any age and would use the programmes and books that I had written. A teacher was in me all of the time. I just needed to focus on myself and ask every day what I could do to help others using my skillset. I am here to teach from a space of love not fear as I did when I had my public practice.

The media loves to play on people's fears but I always focus on what is best for myself. When I held a financial awareness for women seminar it was amazing how many women left their financial affairs to their partners. Also, the number of women who were in blended relationships and had no idea how to protect their assets. Once you can take control of your life, it all becomes a lot simpler and you will be at peace knowing that all is in order.

In summary, I can now say that menopause is a wonderful time of my life. I am living it on my terms and not focusing on people who are not willing to take responsibility for themselves. The freedom I have every day knowing that I can help those who want to be helped is more powerful than running around trying to rescue people. I am happy with the body shape I now have and have discovered that not every man wants a size 10 girl. They want one that has a big smile and is happy on the inside. A lot of hard work has been done with raising a family and now it is my time for fun. I am planning on having a trip to LA in September to be a sponsor at the Emmy Awards and I am going to share the experience with my daughter. What an amazing opportunity for both of us. That is life you never know what is around the corner but it is up to you to choose the direction and make the choices that align with how you want your story to pan out.

Cheryl Field

PointClickCare
Principal Product Manager

www.linkedin.com/in/cherylfield1621
https://www.facebook.com/profile.php?id=61564158076135
https://www.instagram.com/cefield50/
https://www.cherylfield.com/

Cheryl Field is a nurse who has worked in healthcare for over 35 years. Along that journey she focused on caring for seniors who needed rehabilitation after hospitalization, and applied that passion to clinical technology companies. Full time Cheryl works on AI in healthcare. After being introduced to IFS Cheryl realized that IFS was able to help her, and other nurses begin healing from professional and personal traumas. Now Cheryl is working IFS into her message. Authoring her first IFS focused chapter in You Can, You Will in 2023, which helped Cheryl to organize her parts and complete a book project she started 10 years ago. Now an International Best-selling author of Prepared! A Healthcare Guide for Aging Adults, Cheryl spends her non-work time speaking at state and national conventions, hospital grand rounds, local libraries, 55+communities and senior centers on a variety of topics related to health care. To learn more about Cheryl and her advocacy visit her website.

My Hot Flashes Don't Need Any Help: A Humorous and Personal Journey Through Menopause

By Cheryl Field

Introduction

It is my belief that women should be educating and empowering other women on the too-often hidden secrets of menopause. We should be getting our information from one another in addition to those healthcare experts who seek to better understand the range of experiences women have facing menopause. As a 57-year-old female, mother of three, and a nurse of 35 years, I have embraced and learned how to be comfortable with lots of intimate human body conversations, so let's get right in it.

Seventy percent of caregivers worldwide are women, and their average age is forty-nine. If you think about what a woman is doing at 49 years old: She may be at the near pinnacle of her career with key leadership roles that come with pressure, long days, and a lot of responsibility in addition to raising children, possibly supporting children up and including through college. At the same time coping with an aging parent who is probably early to mid-70s ranging too early to mid-80s and starting to have changes in health that require supportive assistance as well as intellectual advocacy. These women are often in intimate relationships with a partner which demands more from their time and energy. On top of all those pressures, these same professional women are coping with the joys of menopause!

As much as some of us women know about menopause, I do not think we share as much institutional knowledge amongst ourselves "as women." I feel like there should be large billboards in life saying, "Look out, perimenopause is sneaking up on you and it is a BEAST." Let me start by saying that by reading more of this chapter you are giving yourself permission to hear my open and honest information sharing. As a 57-year-old menopausal woman I hear you, I see you, I feel you, and I hope that in this chapter by sharing some of what I have learned, I can help to inform you. I also tend to look at life through a lens of humor so I might even entertain you! I am going to share my personal experience as the chapter title suggests one aspect of menopause, **THE HEAT** of the matter.

Menopause, the end of a woman's reproductive years, is often marked by a notorious symptom – hot flashes. Sometime in my mid-forties, I was riding in a friend's car and the seat warmers were on. I think seat warmers have become somewhat of an up-and-coming feature in new cars. All my friends were getting them! Innocently I would jump into a car, and within a few moments, I started to feel like I wanted to jump out of the car! It was about that time that the title of this chapter "My Hot flashes don't need any help" became one of my frequent sayings. There were so many unexpected triggers of hot flashes in the everyday world – nothing anyone ever warned me about. So, let me say it again, our hot flashes do not need any help, however women do! This chapter aims to shed light on the triggers of hot flashes and provide practical tips to manage them effectively, all while keeping a sense of humor about the whole sweaty ordeal. Before we get into the "heat of the matter" I will share that, for me, my hot flashes are not all about the heat.

My hot flashes began as a light sensation of a tingle in my spine upon awakening. I remember thinking, oh this is not so bad. This went on for several months and I began to think I was going to be the lucky one who had morning flashes and nothing else. As time went on, I began to have Hollywood-style hot flashes "everywhere." The thing is – before any change in temperature begins for me, I have what I describe as the "fidgets" – an uncontrollable need to move around, reposition, stop whatever I am doing, and do something else. This fidget moment comes with some nausea, and precedes a hot flash for me every time. It is still to this day an uncontrollable urge to reposition, try not to toss my lunch, and oh have I mentioned I **must move**! It is not always easy or convenient to simply get up and move around. I find myself seat belted on airplanes, sitting on video conference calls, mourning at a funeral when suddenly this internal urge, no, not an urge, it is like a rage, it is a need that cannot be denied and it is telling me to get up, move, go! Suddenly in the most awkward moments, yes, even the most intimate of moments, every cell in my body becomes dedicated to changing positions and moving around. Then comes that nausea, all before any heat. That internal force is amazing to me. I had no idea that my body could conjure up so much demand, so quickly. Frankly, I am a little pissed off that despite the powerful energy that comes before a hot flash, followed by nausea, these moments do not require any calories, as I have managed to only gain weight in this phase of my life. That could be another whole other chapter. Over time I have come to appreciate my fidget moments – at least I knew what was coming next – fleeting nausea and the HEAT of the matter was on deck.

Those innocent tingling sensations that gently woke me from sleep changed into what I described earlier as "Hollywood-style hot flashes." The fidgets were my warning, and I became appreciative of them. At this time in my career, I was working as a Chief Product Officer at a mid-sized start-up. As a nurse, I moved out of direct care after 15 years and moved into clinical informatics roles focused on senior care providers. The healthcare world was getting off paper and into the digital process, and being a nurse working on the technology side of the problem was exhilarating. This role brought me and my perimenopausal self to some meetings and moments I will never forget. Controlling the fidget moments in a customer meeting was one of the first awkward challenges I faced. My clients were accepting of my "need to stand up from time to time" which I associated with "back arthritis" which was far more comfortable for me to share publicly. When at the corporate office as I felt the fidgets come on, I would excuse myself and head out of a boardroom to the ladies' room before the waterworks began. I will share later in this chapter my techniques which I would use once in the restroom to reduce the discomfort of the whole fidget plus hot flash experience.

Okay, so here I was in my late forties, coping with my fidget moments and hot flashes thinking this will end "soon." I was thinking like 3–6 months. My scientific approach and nursing training made me think as estrogen levels depleted and the monthly cycle stopped that all the symptoms of menopause would stop. I was very wrong. I did not realize even as I entered perimenopause that the change of life might last for the rest of my life. If you are like me, you might be thinking you would have a flash here and there, your menstrual cycle would stop, and would go on into those golden years where someday being a widowed grandmother would be the pinnacle of my existence! I was very wrong! I got up the courage to talk to my sister who was three years older than me about her experience. It really hit me – she was STILL having hot flashes. I recall the conversation in detail: I asked her when her hot flashes had started and when they had stopped. I was shocked to learn they were still going strong! Ladies, it is going to be YEARS to make this transition. My advice is to pack up your turtlenecks and sweaters, invest in tank tops, and only button or zippered layers! Getting undressed faster than a horney teenager is a menopausal sport you will be training for – for years!

Personal Story: The Unexpected Triggers

Now, let's talk about triggers. You might think spicy food or a muggy day would be the culprits, but oh no, life is not that simple. I want to share here some of the unexpected triggers of hot flashes that I experienced and later found out that others were experiencing too. Educating each other, empowering one another, and getting it out in the open, as common knowledge among women is my goal for writing this chapter. Social media does make tons of "content" easily accessible if you know what you are looking for, and if the content is authentic, honest, and if you are comfortable talking about some uncomfortable stuff.

Let me tell you about the time I went for my annual mammogram. There I was, standing half-naked in a chilly room, trying to engage in small talk with the technician who would be doing my mammogram. She was instructing me on the required contorted position I would need to get into in order for my breast tissue to be flat on the plate without a single cell of adjacent fat interfering with the images. As technicians do, she gently lifted my breast and at the same time moved my shoulder closer to the machine when BAM I was hit by the fidgets... I knew what was coming. She had my breast in her hand guiding it forward while every other cell in my body wanted to move away and I knew what was next: the sweaty cold clammy hot flash. I swear, the technician must have thought I was having a meltdown. It was of course really embarrassing to me. I started to apologize and explain that I was not ready for her to press that plate down. My voice was clearly full of panic, and distress when the technician stopped me and said – "Don't worry this happens all the time." I was like really? REALLY?? REALLY!! Here I was facing the mammogram machine with all the anxiety THAT brings, fighting my fidget, in an exposed and vulnerable position and this could have been part of the brochure! Part of the inner circle of knowledge we share among women! How is it we do not share this information with other women in advance?! Here is the secret no one told me – physical touch may trigger your hot flashes! A hug from a friend, a pat on the back, that casual hand-on-the-shoulder gesture of support, and yes, the touches that are a part of foreplay, intimacy, sex, whatever words you use. Bottom line – touching can turn into a sweaty ordeal in a 'flash." From the grips of the mammogram machine, you too might generate the heat that helps you slip out of the hands of veteran technicians! Now you know my most uncomfortable trigger but there are more we should reveal so you can share among your circle of women colleagues.

Top 10 Triggers of Hot Flashes

While the exact cause of hot flashes is not fully understood, certain factors are known to trigger them:

1. Hormonal Changes: According to the Mayo Clinic (www.mayoclinic.org), hot flashes, which are the most common symptom of menopause, are primarily triggered by the decline in estrogen levels. This hormonal change makes the hypothalamus, the body's thermostat, more sensitive to slight variations in body temperature. As a result, the hypothalamus initiates a series of events to cool the body down, leading to the sensation we call a hot flash. On average, hot flashes symptoms persist for more than seven years. Some women have them for more than 10 years. If you were thinking three to six months like I was… Well, now you know!

2. Heat (Heated car seats, hot airplanes, and spicy foods): Remember your thermostat the hypothalamus is more sensitive to ever so slight variations in temperature. One might argue that it is a bit overactive, so let us do all we can to avoid micro changes in temperature.

3. Alcohol: Even though you are enjoying a frozen margarita, the alcohol can trigger hot flashes. Here is how that works. When alcohol is consumed, it can cause blood vessels near the skin's surface to dilate, leading to a sensation of warmth. This

dilation, known as vasodilation, can increase body temperature ever so slightly and trigger hot flashes.

4. Caffeine: Even your iced coffee (if it has caffeine) can trigger hot flashes due to its stimulating effects on the central nervous system. Caffeine can accelerate your heart rate, raise your blood pressure, and increase your body temperature and we learned that our body is overly sensitive to micro changes in temperature. Additionally, caffeine's vasoconstrictive properties can cause blood vessels to constrict and then dilate, leading to fluctuations in body temperature, another trigger for the hypothalamus.

5. Stress and Anxiety: The Cleveland Clinic (https://health. clevelandclinic.org) explains that stress or anxiety can trigger hot flashes due to the body's "fight or flight" response. Under stress, your body releases hormones like adrenaline and cortisol, which increase your heart rate and blood flow to muscles. This response can cause a sudden sensation of heat, and we have learned that your body does not like these slight changes in temperature.

6. Smoking: It can trigger hot flashes due to its impact on your heart and hormone levels. Like caffeine, the nicotine in cigarettes increases the heart rate and causes blood vessels to constrict and then dilate, leading to fluctuations in body temperature. Additionally, smoking can affect estrogen levels, which also play a critical role in regulating body temperature.

7. Touch: As mentioned in the mammogram experience, touch can trigger the same "fight or flight" hormonal response, which leads to changes in heart rate, body temperature, and BAM...hot flashes.

8. Diet Pills and Certain Medications: They may also trigger hot

flashes. If you think about the active ingredients in the medications you are taking that interact with hormones, body temperature, or heart rates will get the same effect, micro changes in body temperature which can trigger the hot flashes.

9. Obesity: In a study published in May 2017 in the journal *Menopause* put out by the North American Menopause Society (NAMS), the experience of hot flashes was found to be intensified in obesity. The connection between obesity and hot flashes is rooted in the amount of additional insulation the body has making it harder to cool off following slight changes in temperature. The insulation makes the distribution of heat more difficult, which then causes obese women to suffer more hot flashes. Monitoring your BMI and taking steps to reduce it may help improve your hot flash experience. I have been clinically obese for most of my life, which may explain why my (fidget + heat = hot flash) experiences were so intense.

Managing Hot Flashes

Managing hot flashes involves mindset, behavior, and routine modifications.

Review the list of common triggers and your own personal situation. Here are some strategies from shared experiences, which you may find helpful.

1. Stay Cool: Keep your environment cool, put the thermostat at a temperature where you are comfortable. For me, at 67 life is good; at 69, my flashes are going crazy! Small portable fans, dipping your hands in cold water in the bathroom, and some essential oils on one's wrists were all methods I used to treat an active hot flash.

2. Promote cool sleep: Get a remote-controlled outlet, plug in an oscillating fan, and turn it on so you can turn the fan on and off from bed using the remote control! My husband gave me this as a gift and although I miss the all-night-long sit-ups routine I used to do to reach the fan controls, this has been my best friend for the past six years.

3. Never wear long sleeves again: Tank tops and lightweight jackets. Dress in layers so you can remove clothing when a hot flash starts. If you are driving the car, take your layer off before you buckle up! It is unsafe to try to remove layers while driving. NOT removing them is not an option, so I have learned to layer down before I buckle up!

4. Control what you can for intake: Limit spicy foods, caffeine, and alcohol or stimulants in medications, especially, in business or more social events. Many of my friends say wine triggers their hot flashes, so switch to soda water and lime add a splash of cranberry, and stay cool!

5. Quit Smoking: Smoking cessation can reduce the frequency and severity of hot flashes.

6. Reduce Unnecessary Stress: Anticipate a hot flash brought on by anxiety. To reduce anxiety over prepare for client meetings, presentations and high-profile meetings so you go in confident, and lessen your risk of a hot flash. Dress in layers and get over the way your arms look in a professional sleeveless top and take that jacket off. Practice deep breathing and manifestations where you see a cool calm presentation.

Conclusion

While hot flashes can be an uncomfortable part of menopause, understanding their triggers and how you can manage them will make you feel more in control. I have been saying no to heated seats, winter coats, and every sweater in my closet for 10 years. As I say often when I am turning down the thermostat or turning on the AC, "my hot flashes don't need any help." The truth is that these minor changes have made my menopause experience more manageable. Of course, every woman's experience with menopause is unique. I am hopeful that sharing some of my experiences and what has worked for me will help you too! This chapter is one senior care nurse's experience and knowledge from my own research. It is important to consult with a healthcare professional for your personalized advice. And most importantly, keep your sense of humor along the way. If you cannot laugh at a hot flash in the middle of a mammogram, when can you?

Carla Wersich

EmpowerHER Hub
Certified Menopause Coaching Specialist & Business Advisor

https://www.facebook.com/CarlaBWersich
https://www.instagram.com/carlawersich/
https://www.carlabwersich.com/

If we haven't met yet, let's change that! I'm Carla Wersich, a momma of 5 (his, mine, and ours) living in a small community in Central Illinois. I transitioned from a Corporate America Manager to a passionate entrepreneur dedicated to empowering women.

As I enter the...pause...I'm not talking about a dramatic story pause, but menopause. Moods shifting, weight gain, brain fog – it's not pleasant, but it's reality. And guess what? This 'ish can last 20 years or more! YIKES!

I'm dedicated to supporting women through this gland finale, mentalpause & embracing the changes together. I'm building EmpowerHER HUB, a vibrant community for women at all stages of menopause, where we can laugh, have fun, and thrive. Join us on this journey to leave mere survival behind and celebrate our transformation with style and grace. I cannot wait for you to dive into this book & share your experiences with us!

Unmasking Menopause: The Raw Truth Begins

By Carla Wersich

It's about to get real. Is that ok with you? I mean, I figured since we are talking about redefining menopause, we can start with how we share about it. So, why not share the real and maybe even the raw? I promise it ends well… What do ya say? Will you stick around to hear more?

Oh, good. If you're reading this, you've decided to hang with me for at least a few more lines.

Let's do some intros, shall we? My name is Carla Wersich (were-sick). I am a momma of 5, a former Corporate America Manager who fell in love with Social Media, Direct Sales, and most importantly empowering women to find their freedom! I turned 50 in August!

Let me tell you the idea of turning 50 was daunting, to say the least. My oldest stepson moved out on his own, my oldest daughter is preparing to move away to college, and well, time, as you know, never stands still. While I still have my other two kiddos at home (16-year-old daughter and 12-year-old son) plus our angel baby, I am filled with regret, sorrow, loneliness, and the feeling of "Is this as good as it gets?" I said it's time for real and raw, but I feel safe here because I know you get what I'm saying.

Hold up for a second and let's back up to where this despair started. You see, I've not always been a regretful person, or even one of doom and gloom. I spent the majority of my life being the happy, witty, and funny gal who didn't let ish bother her. As of late, that girl has been in the witness protection program. I mean - she's gone! I went from a super confident, highly successful business badass to someone who didn't want to leave her home. Didn't want to be social. Didn't want to drive. It was crippling. But that's not how it started...

Picture this: Sicily (just kidding, but did anyone follow me for a second with my GG reference?) Seriously though, I was alone at home and uh hmmm...otherwise disposed. Ok, ok - I was using the potty. Then all of a sudden this rush of LAVA-level heat came from my toes, up into my belly - moving its way to my neck. My thoughts LEGIT were - "This is it, I'm ending my days right here on the pot." I was close enough to a wall that I let my head rest there until I met my maker. It lasted only a few seconds. Once it was all said and done - I was like what in the SAM HELL just happened? Then it occurred to me - OMG, that was a hot flash/flush.

That first hot flash felt like my body was betraying me. I had always prided myself on being in control, but she had different plans. It forced me to confront my fears and insecurities in a way I never had before.

Even with the hot flash, it NEVER occurred to me that I was entering..."THE CHANGE." One reason is I've never had another hot flash since that one - well, at least at the time I am writing this chapter anyway...check on your girl - I may be in a corner melting as you read this.

Next up - I was leaving on a jet plane. Man oh man - I'm really dating myself here - or maybe it's because I had "older parents." Yeah, that's my story. Anyway, headed to the airport after attending a company conference. Traveling alone - which used to be a treat and now it's just an anxiety-ridden experience. You too? Oh, good. Not the only one here.

Well, my Aunt Flo was with me. I was prepared, or so I thought. I made it through security and trying to find my gate when the gates of hell opened up and massive flooding came upon me. I couldn't get to the bathroom quickly enough. Ladies who've given birth - this was similar to the first time standing up after delivering your babe. That kind of emergency situation. I spent the next 2 hours in and out of the bathroom praying I could make it home without looking like I was straight out of a gorey Halloween movie. I know, it's TMI, but stick with me. You ever have situations like this where you think - ah, this hasn't happened before so I will just wait and see what happens next? Yeah, that was me - let's just wait this out.

Fast-forward a year or so when massive heart palpitations started making their way into my world. My family has a serious history of heart disease so I did not take this lightly. I spoke with my practitioner and she ordered some tests and I had to wear a heart monitor for 24 hours.

I don't know why I feel it's important to state this, but I'm not one to visit a doctor unless I feel it's serious OR it's my normal routine lab work as a type 2 diabetic.

Anyway, can you guess what came of the monitoring? Nothing. No abnormalities. All tests came back normal. Yet, I felt like my heart would beat right out of my chest. I tried some modifications at home, but it didn't work. Over time, they dissipated.

And so did the heavy bleeding...or again...so I thought. Nope - that came back with a vengeance. So bad that I was nervous to leave the house. I knew it was time to have it checked out. Battery of tests, ultrasound, etc., - guess what they found? YUP - ZILCH, NADA - all came back normal. While I was relieved, I was still confused. My body is telling me it's not NORMAL.

Enter random shoulder pain...on my left side that was bad enough, it would wake me up at night. I was popping Ibuprofen and Tylenol like candy. X-rays, exams, etc., - nah...you're good. There isn't anything wrong. Must be a muscle sprain of some sort.

OHHHH, and let's not forget that I mysteriously started gaining weight rapidly in my mid-section without any changes to my diet. It felt like it packed on overnight.

I was getting super frustrated with my brain also not functioning like it used to. I couldn't complete sentences, would completely forget conversations, appointments, and on occasion to pick up a kid!

It felt like all at once my world was crumbling. I just thought, well, I am getting older so this must just be as good as it gets. But something was telling me to dig a little deeper.

So, what do ya do? You GTS, of course. Ya know - Google That S...tuff. Tell me I'm not alone in the self-diagnosing. I'm not encouraging it - get the stuff checked out by a medical professional, but if you're like me, you go immediately to WWW to get some answers.

Time and time again, the results came back about menopause. But, wait - I'm not having night sweats, I'm not having hot flashes - this cannot be menopause.

To my surprise, I was experiencing more and more symptoms of menopause. Mood swings, sleep disturbances, fatigue, brain fog, low energy. Turns out every single one of the issues I was having could be a result of perimenopause.

So, I began doing more research. Yes, I could find studies that showed results about what you may experience in menopause, but what I couldn't find was how to treat it and more importantly, finding other women who were open to sharing their experiences!

That's when I decided, if I (the open book that I am) didn't know what to expect during this phase of my life, and felt so alone as I was uncovering it - there have to be many other women who are feeling isolated and alone as well. That has to change!

So, I dove into learning. I found a program for which I could become a certified menopause specialist. I certified for myself so I would be better equipped with tools and resources for my own journey. Who knows, this may lead to helping women like you too!

But as I started to implement some of the changes in nutrition to recognize what my body needed (and didn't), things changed. One of the biggest game-changers for me was using a Continuous Glucose Monitor. Oftentimes, it's prescribed for diabetics to monitor blood sugar, but it is incredibly helpful in general to learn and know how your body responds to food. I can see in real time if my body is going to love or hate the food I put into it.

For me, lowering my carb intake and reducing the amount of processed foods, added more leafy greens and healthy fats. Within weeks, my energy levels increased, and the brain fog started to lift. HALLELUJAH - cause that meno-brain is no joke!

I'm still hanging onto the unexpected 20-pound weight gain in my middle region…but baby steps, right? Maybe we can work on that together? Yeah, let's do that - it's a date!

Ahh, now I'm all up in my feelings - speaking of which, I didn't expect these overwhelming feelings of disappointment. The immense feeling of regret, of not doing enough, of not being a good mother - it all boils down to "Is this as good as it gets?" Almost grieving the loss of my youth, of a social life, or some days just sad. Like, did I get IT right…whatever IT is?

As I attempted to process these feelings, I felt such a strong pull that I was about to embark on something bigger. I was meant to share my story, even when it may be a bit much - it's the real deal.

I was meant to be someone who can and will empower women to share their own struggles with a community of like-minded women, but to feel strong in their own voice to say - ya know, this doesn't feel right. To listen to their own body when something feels off and to not settle for - "at your age" this is what happens. Maybe that's the truth - but we know there are alternatives, we know there are solutions that can help us manage the journey we are on - even if we are just starting, or seeing the light at the end of the tunnel - we need each other.

I am not claiming to be the ULTIMATE expert in the field of menopause solutions, but I am committed to finding and sharing resources, experts, and testimonials from others who have navigated or are navigating the pause victoriously.

I am building a community of women celebrating women. A place where women can safely share their craziest stories, look for someone who gets her, find resources not only to help guide them during the change, but also all the other changes that come with aging - empty nest, sexual wellness, retirement (and now what) and you betta believe she will laugh her menopausal belly off. I'm proud to say, I have created just that for you.

I would love to invite you to join EmpowerHER HUB, your ultimate destination for embracing life's transitions with style and grace! 💥 Embark on our Road Trip to Reinventing Menopause and Life Beyond 40, where we navigate the twists and turns of menopause, an empty nest, and the everyday challenges of being bold and beautiful beyond 40. This community is here for you with tips, support, and lots of laughs - I think you can tell I love to laugh and help others do the same!

I cannot wait to see you on the inside! As you prepare to turn the page, know that I am cheering you on throughout this book. I pray that you find exactly what you need from these pages from these amazing women. Thank you for taking time to read my story. Much love to you!

Virginia Walters

Author

https://www.facebook.com/people/Virginia-Oracle/61559259616939/?mibextid=LQQJ4d
https://www.instagram.com/virginiaellenpsychicreader/

At 52, Virginia Walters, a Sydney resident, has triumphed over significant health challenges. Diagnosed with ovarian tumours and endometrial cancer, polycystic ovarian syndrome, Virginia underwent surgical menopause, enduring severe complications including torsion and necrosis of the ovaries, which nearly claimed her life. In the face of these trials, she discovered meditation as a powerful tool for managing menopausal symptoms. By harnessing the energy of hot flushes and redirecting it creatively, Virginia cultivated her intuition and developed clairvoyant and mediumistic abilities. For over 15 years, she has practiced daily meditation, which has become a cornerstone of her healing journey and personal growth. Virginia now shares her insights and experiences, inspiring others to explore meditation, spiritual development as a path to emotional and spiritual well-being.

Redefining Menopause

By Virginia Walters

In 2013, I was taken to hospital by ambulance for emergency surgery. What was shown via ultrasound to be cysts the size of an orange on the ovaries turned out to be 3 litres of tumours attached to them; these tumours had spread through my bowels and abdomen. The leading surgeons weren't sure what they were dealing with and couldn't provide clarity until they went in surgically and could explore what was happening. However, the leading surgeon reassured me that the surgical team was doing everything possible to save my ovaries, even if it was just one or a half of one, that they would do their best.

As I was lying, waiting on the operating bed to be anesthetised, an older man walked through the operating theatre doors. Walking up to me, he introduced himself as the head of the oncology gynaecology department. He asked me several questions before saying,"I'm not going to save your ovaries today; I'm not even going to attempt to save your ovaries. I will remove them, but in doing so, I will save your life." He continued, "I'm tired of seeing women come in year after year with the same issue and eventually losing them to ovarian cancer." I felt an eternal rush of gratitude wash over me. I was so grateful to have found myself in his care. I replied, "I'm not attached to my ovaries; they have given me four children. I would rather my children have a mother than myself have ovaries."

Thankfully, during the surgery, the surgeon could drain these tumours and begin seeing where they originated from and what they were doing. It seemed that I had the polycystic ovarian syndrome, which had caused the cysts to form, grow, and eventually turn into tumours. There was torsion of both ovaries; both were necrotic, and one had evidence of gangrene. I was in a bad state; there was no other option available than to remove both ovaries. I underwent an oophorectomy. It was discovered under biopsy that the ovaries had what is known to be serious borderline tumours. It was the beginning stage of ovarian cancer. This surgery saved my life. I felt incredibly blessed to have been given a second chance at life, although I would need monitoring. I was given a 5-year window before I would be entirely out of the woods. The statistics that I was looking at were a 10% chance of cancer returning during the first three years, followed by a 5% change over the next two years; then, I would be clear for life.

In the coming days, I sat with stillness. I had somehow miraculously cheated death and couldn't help but wonder what this meant. While still in the hospital, my eldest son came to see me, bringing the news that an American agency had scouted him and that there was an opportunity for him to play soccer professionally. I marvelled; had I not landed into the capable hands of this medical team, my son would have been attending my funeral rather than attending an interview for an international scholarship. I felt incredibly blessed to have survived and to be with my children. I began to think about life. My life. My values. Ethic. Belief systems and what it means to live a good life and be a good person. I concluded that I wasn't perfect, and of course, I had regrets, challenges, obstacles, and disappointments; however, on the balance of things, I felt that I had done enough, had been enough, and was good enough. Still, what would this mean?

In the following weeks, my body experienced shock due to this sudden hormone change. In typical circumstances, menopause would be a gradual process beginning with perimenopause before transitioning into menopause. This process typically takes place over years; however, since I underwent the process surgically rather than organically, placing me into a menopausal state instantly. My body didn't quite know how to process what was happening.

It began as an intense heat rise within my body, starting somewhere in my midsection, sending heart palpitations before settling into my face, causing a hot feeling and sweating around my neck, head, and face. This feeling was disorientating, uncomfortable, and quite overwhelming. Additionally, I felt tenderness with swelling and pain throughout my breasts; oddly, I began lactating.

Fearing the worst, I asked my GP to refer me to a breast physician specialist, where I was examined. Interestingly, the doctor never once looked at my breasts; instead, using only the tips of their fingers, skilfully felt for changes in tissue texture, which often occurs in cases where tumours are present. Again, it seemed that I had landed in expert hands. The specialist reassured me that the changes I was experiencing were due to the oophorectomy and hormone changes. It appeared that the sudden changes in hormones due to the surgical menopause had confused my brain chemistry. The brain's logic was to interpret this as me being pregnant and thus beginning the process of accommodating a baby by producing breast milk. The specialist reassured me that this would settle down over the coming months, that the ducts would eventually dry out and atrophy, that the breast tissue would change too, and that my breasts would go through the natural occurrence that breasts go through with menopause. I felt a little sad about this; however, it was a small price. I felt that same wave of gratitude wash over me and the incredible blessing I had received. I had cheated death and had been given another chance at life.

My hormones and brain chemistry weren't the only things that confused me; I questioned everything. I found myself experiencing an existential crisis. I was a single parent studying towards a double degree in law and social sciences. Several years earlier, I'd returned to school, completing my high schooling before earning the grades to qualify for university studies. I'd always had a strong sense of justice and a desire for goodness and purpose with an agility of spirit. The most significant part of me yearned to become a human rights lawyer. You see, my youngest had a profound form of cerebral palsy, and over time, I found myself becoming more and more involved with advocating for a fairer system. However, this now all seemed irrelevant. It would have died with me. What had been a dream come true now began to fade. What emerged was an intense knowingness to sit with stillness. It was a force that was greater than me.

I wasn't sure where life was leading me, but I felt this force calling me to meditate. I was familiar with meditation, which I had been doing daily for about five or six years. It was my morning routine. After getting the kids up and off to school, I would sit quietly for the next hour and a half, silently meditating before writing my diary, tracking thoughts, my use of time, and goals. Then, I would begin my studies. I had this strong desire that would fuel me like a fire; I felt this diminish; the drive wasn't there anymore. However, it had become replaced with an incredible sense of desire. The drive turned to desire, a more focused, purposeful energy. Rather than a pull, it became a longing. My priorities began to shift, and genuine soul-searching emerged. It wasn't like the soul-searching journey I'd been on up until this point of figuring out who I was and how I fit into the world. It was more of making peace with myself at a soul level. An intense stillness, like I was witnessing life as a spectator, observing and being truly present in the conversation. More focused on the now, the moment, this moment. This moment, there is. I am this moment. I am my own.

Where there had been a focus on becoming, I now felt it was essential just to be. I grew ambivalent about everything other than my relationship with my children up until that point. However, there was a place for this new ambivalence, and it was necessary to sit with it to make it my friend and to feel what it wanted to teach me. What I felt emerging was the crone, that wise woman that resides deep within. She needed space, time, and energy to allow her to appear, and what followed can be described as the Lotus that grows in the depths of mud and despair before growing and fully becoming a flower. I felt this in my personal life, goals, and relationships with family, friends, and partners. I went from a single mother to a sole parent; other than my children, the rest of the world could fade until I made peace with what had been and what was to come. I wondered what this might mean. I concluded that I didn't need to know, only that life would show me moment by moment, day by day. I would continue to be.

It was a sad day to withdraw from university. As I queued up and waited for my turn in the administrative office, I held myself with courage. As I handed the paperwork in, I felt like I was saying goodbye to my life, the life I'd been living until this point in time, and somehow failed. I silently prayed for the people I would have liked to help in the future and prayed for those who would study and go on to help these people. It didn't feel this was enough; it only needed to be enough.

My morning meditation practice quickly became 3 hours of daily meditation. I also slept a lot. Before being admitted to the hospital, I had migraine and fibromyalgia. I had come so close to death, and I still had another five years of monitoring before I would statistically have the all-clear. My daily meditation practice was helping with this; however, I was chronically tired and needed soul rest. Interestingly, the phenomena occurring throughout my body from an observational perspective were incredible. I began to meditate through the experience and follow the energy as it moved throughout my being.

I would feel an intense heat rise throughout my body. It would start somewhere in my midsection or solar plexus region. I would feel it rise through my stomach and chest before reaching my head and creating a moment of confusion or disorientation. I would sweat profusely during these moments. My hair clung to my face and neck with sweat. It was quite discomforting. I later discovered that this is what was called a hot flush.

The hot flushes brought about changes and sensations that I could not escape, and although they could be disorientating, I decided to welcome this new energy; I travelled through my body through my mind's eye, observing it rather than avoiding or fearing it. I sat with it. I asked about its purpose and what it had to teach me. For me, it felt similar to the rush before an orgasmic climax. An all-encompassing wave of disorientating, heated energy rose throughout my being. However, to me, it didn't feel sexual but rather purposeful. There was a rising of what felt like creative energy, an efflux calling me into a different state of being. This energy felt more purposeful as some inner aspect of myself wanted to emerge. Slowly, she revealed herself as the crone. The emergence of the crone was elevating my consciousness through the rise of the hot flush. It felt like a spiritual elevation rather than a sexual one. However, I've heard other women use this energy to re-energise and give a second life to their sexuality. I guess for some, the inner cougar emerges beside the crone. I sat with it and meditated through the experience, bringing me to a higher level of consciousness. A private sacredness emerged, and I felt like I was my own. I began to see my sexuality as my own and an extension of who I am. As a heterosexual woman, the male counterpart does not necessarily activate it or stimulate it. Upon reflection, I felt somewhat dissatisfied with the mechanical feel-good process of sex and a more profound calling for sacred union. I felt a deep desire to blend or emerge with a holy bond and, therefore, needed to step away from anything that didn't mirror that. From there, I entered into a relationship with the workings of spirit and a type of pause. It was calling me into stillness and calmness. I felt blessed that I had the luxury of doing this without a partner. The thought of processing the experience through another and the effect on them was unimaginable. I felt grateful to go through this experience alone and process these changes. I wanted to know that energy well before I could open up and share it with another. It was like my body, essence, and soul paused; I knew and felt a calling to wait for a sacred union, the right person. The sexual drive that I previously felt, through this inner work, became a deep desire for a holy union with the right person for him and me. I knew to adopt a space of celibacy; this best suited me.

Beyond that, I felt a deep calmness and a feeling of disconnection from the world to the busyness and productive energy that seemed to govern me previously. I would observe this energy and the creativeness of what it was and ask for direction. I began to delve into sculpture and textile arts. I was meditating for inspiration before creating each stage, asking the art what it wanted to be and how it wanted to look. As a small child creating dolls with my grandmother, I remember her words, "She will tell you how she wants to look, and it will not be how you want her to look. Just see it in your mind, then put your vision into reality." I recall my great-grandmother and mother also creating similarly. I was stepping into my maternal lineage through this energy. I was using this creative menopausal energy to make art, bringing through the teachings of my elders and adding my inspiration. With initial hesitation, I began exhibiting my art and was shocked when I won several awards with them. I donated one that is now permanently displayed at the oncology gynecology clinic.

Other things were happening, too, and my intuitive ability began to heighten. I had always been an intuitive person; however, I found that almost as if overnight, it had increased, gathering momentum as I meditated. I would see here and know things. I found this rather curious and had quite a few exciting adventures; for example, while in meditation, a spirit being showed an object and where to find it. Curiously, I decided to travel to the place where I had seen the object. When I arrived there and looked around, I found it. It was amazing. It blew my mind how these things could happen when other things began. I discovered that when I would hold an object, it was like I could read its energy—the same with people. If I held their hand, it was like suddenly I could have access to information about them that I hadn't known 5 minutes before.

I would go into more profound meditations and follow the energy of my body and what the energy was saying to me. It was through this that I saw the cancer in my uterus. Had the cancer returned, or was it there all along? I didn't know. I only knew that I had seen it and that I now needed a hysterectomy. I went back to the clinic and asked for a biopsy. The biopsy concluded that there were cellular changes; however, there were no signs of cancer. The doctor recommended that, given my history, I undergo a total hysterectomy. Unfortunately, during the surgery, there were complications, and I suffered a hemorrhage. Given my rare blood type, I wasn't able to have a transfusion; however, the surgeon put me on bed rest with a drip for several weeks. The biopsy found stage one cancer throughout the endometrium. Fortunately, it was detected early enough that surgery was sufficient. However, this added another 10% chance over another five years of cancer returning, meaning that if all went well, I would go into clear in February 2020. I busied myself with my grandchildren from my eldest daughter and spent as much time focused on my children building successful lives as possible; my youngest daughter excelled in leadership roles, and my son built several businesses before finding his niche. My youngest child would remain an eternal child within a profoundly compromised body. All I could do was love him and navigate his life so that he would have access to the best care and experiences that brought him as much joy as possible for as long as we were here.

As my intuition continued to grow and develop, I wanted to extend that outwards, to assist people wherever possible, so I applied for a few fairs and started reading occasionally. It became like a hobby and a new way of meeting people with similar abilities. I did this for a few years, and then one day in 2018, I was in a second-hand store when I saw a framed tapestry. Although it was unknown to me at the time, it was a hand-stitched A3 size copy tapestry of the lady and the unicorn; I instantly fell in love with it as it reminded me of the 9 of the Pentacles tarot card, a card that often represents myself. I purchased it and brought it home. Then, I received a phone call from a manager of a local homeware store a few weeks later asking me whether I was available to do an in-store event. I happily agreed. To my delight and surprise, when I arrived at work that day, the store had a tent almost identical to the one in the tapestry. I continued to read out of that tent, which quickly became known as the tent of secrets up until 2021. It was a fantastic experience. I met so many wonderful people. It inspired me to study community work, case management, and psychology/social work and write and educate wherever possible. I still conduct clairvoyant readings and training towards channelling. I also create, paint, garden, crochet, and restore furniture, basically whatever I feel driven towards. If I could share one message about menopause with women, it would be to allow the process to take you where your soul needs to go and that this doesn't change who you are; instead, it refines and directs you into an authentic way of being within the world. With much love, all the way from Australia, Virginia Walters x

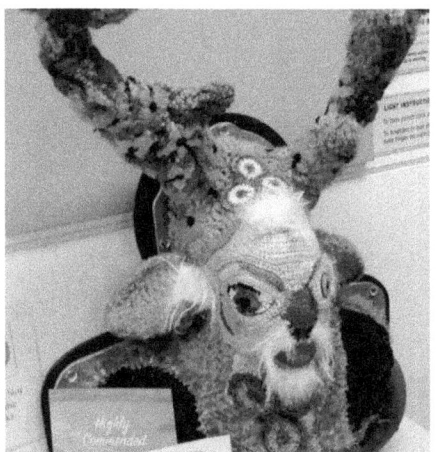

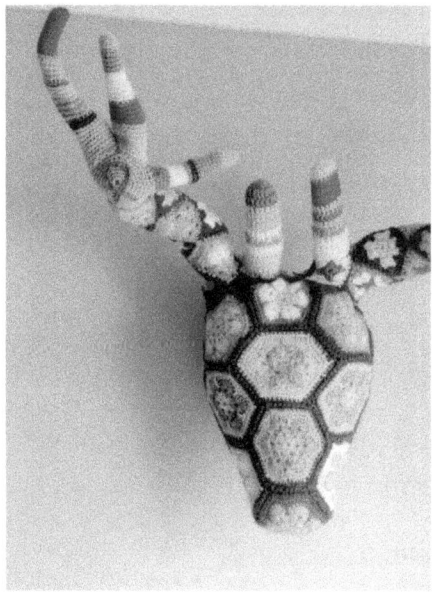

'SCHMOONIE'

The message the reindeer totem carries is faith. It's about learning to take a leap of faith into the unknown and placing one's trust in the process of life rather than an outcome. In a sense, the focus becomes about the journey. Similarly, the journey one takes following a cancer diagnosis could be considered comparable in essence. The ongoing monitoring, treatment and uncertainty which often follows a cancer diagnosis is comparable to the message Reindeer brings – that is, to trust the process.

The antlers represent the 'fight' which is often associated with cancer. Whether that is the fight which the surgeon faces navigating through a long and difficult surgery when things don't go as planned, the nursing and hospital staff's consistency and kindness or the caregivers who support their loved one, they each face their own battles. Together they fight the good fight.

The sculpture was deliberately made without ears. Gynaecological cancers are often referred to as silent killer as symptoms are often subtle and are not often heard until they reach a more advanced stage.

The colours used are representative of women's gynaecological cancer and each flower represents a different form of cancer.

Teal = ovarian cancer, fallopian tube cancer

Peach = endometrial, uterine cancer

Blue and white = cervical cancer

Pink = cervical cancer

Mauve = vulva cancer

Purple = all gynaecological cancers

Yellow = hope

The Reindeer was sculptured by hand using paper, wire, tape and plaster. The cover is hand crocheted using 100% merino wool. Patterns used are traditional granny squares, African daisy motifs and freeform crochet to bring it all together.

Fernanda Lima Firman

Summit To Launch
Events Profit Architect & Online Business Consultant

https://www.linkedin.com/in/felimafirman/
https://www.facebook.com/fefirman/
https://www.instagram.com/fernanda.firman/
https://www.fernandafirman.com/
https://www.summittolaunch.com/

I am a Brazilian architect turned AI Automations strategist and producer behind some of the most popular 6-figure launches and visibility-driven Summits online!

Many people don't realize that technology has become so advanced that it can do much of the work for you but I also know how overwhelming tech can be, and I've been in that place myself so I am here to help you implement, organize, automate and streamline this process.

My mission is to simplify AI and automations in your business (and personal life) so you can be more productive, increase profitability, reduce stress and spend more time doing the things you love and bring you joy.

If you would like to learn how you can leverage AI and Automations to grow your business or systemize your personal life, I prepared a few gifts for you:

1. A free audit of your business
2. Download a list of the most popular prompts I use.

https://www.fernandafirman.com/airesources
or scan the QR code below.

Embracing Change: From Guilt to Purpose

By Fernanda Lima Firman

When I was growing up in Brazil, menopause wasn't something anyone ever talked about. The only thing I knew was that it meant you were getting old and could no longer have kids since your periods would stop. In a place where men often left their wives for younger women, the fear of aging was deeply ingrained in our culture.

I considered myself strong and confident, believing I was immune to these fears. But without realizing it, I carried these lessons with me across the miles and years, even after starting a new life in America.

Happily married, mother to two incredible boys, running a successful six-figure business, and homeschooling my children while working from home, I built a fulfilling life. My social life was vibrant—Brazilians love to party, and my weekends were always filled with social events.

My life was full, busy, and satisfying…until one day, it wasn't.

The Subtle Onset

The first signs of perimenopause were so subtle that I almost missed them. I began to forget things and felt a fog settle over my mind, creating a hazy confusion that made even the simplest tasks feel monumental. Tasks that once took hours began stretching into half a day or more. I double-checked everything, terrified I'd forget something important.

Night after night, I woke up drenched in sweat, my heart pounding, and with an unbearable headache. I attributed it all to stress—I was pushing hard at work, managing multiple online launches, running 3 virtual summits, building robust automation systems, and learning about AI.

Of course, I was tired. Of course, I was stressed. But deep down, I knew it was more than that as the signs became impossible to ignore.

Struggling Behind the Scenes

As a high achiever, I've always thrived under pressure. My career journey from international architect and project manager to online launch strategist, summit producer, and AI-driven automation expert demanded high focus and attention to detail.

I partner with my clients to plan, strategize, and execute their events online, often juggling multiple projects simultaneously. I prided myself on always over-delivering.

But behind the scenes, I worked twice as hard to keep everything on track. The harder I worked, the more anxious I became, leading to sleepless nights. My once-sharp mind felt dull, and the crushing anxiety made me doubt my skills and everything I had built over the years.

How could I be good at what I do if I couldn't even think straight?

Impact at Home and on Relationships

At home, things weren't any better. My husband, always my biggest cheerleader and partner in everything, seemed distant and confused by the changes he saw in me. I was gaining weight despite my best efforts, and his well-intentioned advice—"Just eat better, exercise more"— only deepened my sense of failure.

Didn't he see that I was trying? Didn't he understand that it wasn't as simple as that? But how could he when even I didn't fully understand what was happening? Moments of frustration and hurt became common between us, adding strain to our once-harmonious relationship.

The lack of sex was a massive point of disconnection for me and my husband. The women around me continued to tell me I needed to satisfy him at home so I would not get cheated on—another cultural belief. He is very sweet but very sexual, and I was tired of denying him. I tried hard to become the sexy woman I was before, but it only led to frustration since my body was failing me. His remarks about the lack of sex really hurt me, and I am sure he was also hurt feeling unwanted.

My periods became so heavy that some days, I couldn't leave the house, afraid I would bleed through my clothes. The regular pads gave me allergic reactions, and the organic ones did not hold the flow. A friend of mine told me about the silicone cups. I would use the cup and an organic pad, but I still had to change it every hour to a couple of hours. That also affected our sexual life.

I started to miss parties, and friends started to be upset by my last-minute cancelations, not understanding that I had no control over my unbearable migraines or when I got my period. Driving long distances and sitting and standing became a moment of anxiety for me. I felt embarrassed to share this.

As the months dragged on, I spiraled into a place I didn't recognize—exhausted, irritable, and prone to tears I couldn't explain. I withdrew from my business, taking on fewer clients. This immediate step back led to a significant drop in income, which added financial strain to the emotional weight I was already carrying and caused issues in my marriage.

The loss of confidence hurt the most, more than the financial hit. I feared I was no longer capable of being the woman I had always been—the woman my husband married, my children depended on, and my clients trusted.

I felt immense guilt for not being the superwoman I had always strived to be.

So, I found myself feeling alone and crying in secret, hiding my tears from my children and my husband, ashamed of what I saw as my failure. I was supposed to be strong, to have it all together, but inside, I was falling apart.

A Moment of Realization

In 2023, I hosted an in-person mastermind event with my friend Jen. I noticed her pulling out a small fan and fanning herself furiously. Sweat was pouring down her face, and she laughed, casually remarking about menopause. The word hit me like a bolt of lightning.

"Jen, are you going through menopause?" I asked.

She nodded with a smile. "Oh yeah, it's like having a furnace inside your body."

At that moment, something clicked. The night sweats, tiredness, brain fog, headaches, weight gain, anxiety—all of it suddenly made sense. *I was going through menopause.*

I remember feeling a jolt of recognition. Jen is younger than me and a woman I admire. Someone who always seemed to have it all together, she was talking openly about something I had been struggling with in silence. I felt a wave of validation. I wasn't alone. This wasn't just me losing my mind—this was something real, something other women were going through, too.

But the relief of this realization was quickly followed by a wave of fear. I was still trying to figure out what to do next.

Seeking Answers and Facing Frustrations

It was Sunday morning in March 2024, and I woke up feeling my worst: shaking, cold, headache, and skipping heartbeats. Something was off, so I went to the ER. As per my previous experiences with

Western medicine, the doctor told me everything was fine and sent me home.

One doctor I saw threatened to call the DMV to revoke my driver's license based on my symptoms of brain fog. Another one insinuated that I was trying to get my husband's attention. And finally, when one of the doctors questioned my ability to care for my children, I became afraid of sharing too much with them. Their solution was always a prescription drug…

Feeling unheard and frustrated after years of misdiagnoses and being told everything was "normal," *I turned to AI*—the same technology I used for my business—to analyze my blood test results based on my symptoms. The AI indicated I had severe untreated anemia over the years and all signs of perimenopause.

Perimenopause? I felt even more lost, having never heard of it before.

Even with all the fear, I wasn't going to let this phase define me. This moment was a turning point, not a dead end.

Finding Support and Taking Control

Determined to find a way forward, I reached out to Angie Spuzak, a client who had hired me to launch her program focused on balancing hormones through food. Angie reviewed my blood tests, pointed out markers traditional doctors had missed, and provided a roadmap to start healing. I immersed myself in resources, leveraging her blog "The Tastes of Life" for recipes and information.

The changes were small at first but powerful. I started paying attention to my body like never before, keeping a journal to note what I ate, slept, and felt each day. I learned to listen to my body's signals and give it what it needed. I cut out alcohol, not because I had to, but because I realized it wasn't serving me.

Allowing myself to take naps during the day was a radical act of self-care for someone who had always prided herself on being an overachiever. I let go of the guilt that had been weighing me down, giving myself permission to rest, slow down, and not be perfect.

In addition to these practical changes, I started to meditate more and introduced moments of prayer into my mornings. This routine grounded me, helping to reduce stress and depression. It allowed me to trust the path I was on, even when things felt uncertain.

Opening Up and Building Understanding

My boys, bright and curious, had noticed the changes in me but didn't understand what was happening. Their once energetic, always-present mom was changing—tired, irritable, and often close to tears for reasons that didn't make sense to them.

I remember hearing my son tell his friend who invited him to a party, "I am not sure I can go. I need to see how my mom will be feeling that day."

It broke my heart, and I knew it was time to talk. They needed to understand menopause and how it affected everything from moods to energy. It was vital for them to know that this wasn't their fault; it was just a phase, a normal part of life.

My husband and I also worked on understanding this phase. I opened up to him about my experiences, and although he's still learning, we're navigating this journey together, one step at a time.

Embracing Positive Changes

As I started to make changes, something incredible happened—I started to feel better. I slept through the night, and the constant anxiety and headaches began to fade.

One morning, I stepped on the scale and saw I had lost twelve pounds without even trying.

More importantly, I started seeing myself differently. I stopped judging my body for the changes it was undergoing and began to embrace and love it as a powerful, resilient vessel that had carried me through so much.

With this new perspective, I also began to make changes in my business. Recognizing that I couldn't continue working the way I had before, I turned to automation and systems that allowed me to step back without losing control. <u>I created systems for everything</u>! I delegated more responsibilities, trusting my team to take more off my plate. This transformation allowed my business to thrive without requiring my constant presence.

Rediscovering Purpose and Empowering Others

Despite the challenges, this journey brought new insights and a renewed sense of purpose.

I shifted my business focus to working with women, helping them create systems that enable them to grow their businesses without stress or burnout. This new direction has been incredibly fulfilling, aligning perfectly with where I am in my life.

I also joined menopause support groups, finding comfort and empowerment in sharing experiences and hearing others' stories. Knowing that I wasn't alone made a world of difference and inspired me to advocate for more open conversations about menopause.

Lessons Learned and Moving Forward

Looking back over the past few years, I see how far I've come—from feeling lost and overwhelmed to finding a new sense of balance and purpose. Menopause is not the end; it's a new chapter filled with growth, strength, and transformation. The wisdom and resilience I've gained through this experience are invaluable.

To every woman reading this, know you don't have to go through this alone. Whether you're just starting to notice the signs of menopause or are deep in the midst of it, there is hope and a way forward that doesn't involve sacrificing your happiness, health, or sense of self.

Start conversations with your children early on. These discussions are about education and building a foundation of empathy and understanding that will carry them into their future relationships.

Let's break the silence together. Let's share our stories, support one another, and redefine what it means to go through menopause—not as something to fear but as a powerful journey of self-discovery and empowerment.

My Key Strategies for Navigating Menopause:

Listen to Your Body:

- *Track What You Eat and How You Feel:* Keep a journal of everything you eat and how you feel afterward. It will help you identify foods that trigger symptoms and make adjusting easier.

- *Prioritize Sleep:* Resist the urge to get up in the middle of the night to check on something. Make sleep a priority because, without it, everything else falls apart.

Give Yourself Grace:

- *Set Realistic Expectations:* Give yourself more time to complete tasks. If something usually takes two days, give yourself four. This reduces pressure and helps manage anxiety.

- *Accept That You Can't Do It All:* Some days, your energy level may be zero. Accept that pushing through may not be the best option. Give yourself permission to rest, even if it means the house is a mess or not everything gets done.

Use Technology to Your Advantage:

- *Automate Where You Can:* Implement automation, AI, and systems in your business to reduce burden and stress and increase efficiency. This allows you to step back when needed without sacrificing quality and profit.

- *Delegate, Lean on your team:* Trust them to handle the details and reassure yourself that everything is under control.

Seek Support:

- *Talk to Friends and Family:* Share what you're going through with your loved ones. Opening up can help bridge gaps and foster understanding.

- *Join a Support Group:* Connect with other women going through menopause. These groups can provide invaluable perspectives and help you feel less isolated.

Find Joy in Small Things:

- *Spend Time Outdoors:* Incorporate more time in the sun and fresh air into your routine. Nature can lift your mood and significantly reduce feelings of depression.

- *Listen to Empowering Music:* Create a playlist of positive, empowering songs. Use this music to shift your mindset on days when you feel overwhelmed or low.

- *Meditate and Pray:* Start your mornings with meditation and moments of prayer. These practices can ground you, reduce stress, and help you trust the path you're on.

Embrace the Change:

- *Love Your Evolving Body:* Appreciate and celebrate your body for its strength and resilience through changes. Focus on appreciating what your body can do, even as it changes. Embrace these changes and recognize the strength and resilience within you.

- ***Focus on the Wisdom Gained:*** Reflect on the wisdom and strength you've accumulated over the years. Understand that these experiences are far more valuable than what you might have had in the past.

Book Cover Artist Credit

Redefining Menopause's front cover art is an acrylic painting 36 by 38 inches canvas called "The Dance". It has about 30 layers and was painted with Golden Fluid Acrylic paint.

The painting represents with its plethora of colors the diversity of women around the world, their dance together, their inclusivity, their unashamed nakedness, their love for their bodies, their free movement, and their freedom from oppression. "The Dance" is a joy-filled celebration of the sisterhood of a post-patriarchal world that honors women's sovereignty over their bodies and their lives. How fitting for "Redefining Menopause"!

The artist is Sylvia Becker-Hill, a German living in Southern California, a Certified Color of Woman Intentional Creativity® Teacher, and the inventor of the Neuro CreativityTM framework in which she combines applied neuroscience, somatic coaching, and new creative forms of painting and drawing to empower lasting transformation in her clients.

If you like the painting and want its juicy, lively, joy-filled energy in your spaces or daily life, gift yourself a print for your walls or on a household item from Sylvia's online store on the Fine Art America platform. You find The Dance print collection behind this link or the QR code below.

If you want to wrap your body with The Dance's frequencies of freedom, order a wearable art fashion piece from Le Galeriste through the QR Code or link below:

https://fineartamerica.com/featured/the-dance-sylvia-becker-hill.html

https://www.legaleriste.com/en/sylvia.becker-hill/The%20Dance-sylvia.becker-hill

For more about Sylvia's art philosophy, online gallery, and painting products, go here:

https://sylviabecker-hill.com/

JOIN THE MOVEMENT!
#BAUW

Becoming An Unstoppable Woman
With She Rises Studios

She Rises Studios was founded by Hanna Olivas and Adriana Luna Carlos, the mother-daughter duo, in mid-2020 as they saw a need to help empower women worldwide. They are the podcast hosts of the *She Rises Studios Podcast* and Amazon best-selling authors and motivational speakers who travel the world. Hanna and Adriana are the movement creators of #BAUW - Becoming An Unstoppable Woman: The movement has been created to universally impact women of all ages, at whatever stage of life, to overcome insecurities, and adversities, and develop an unstoppable mindset. She Rises Studios educates, celebrates, and empowers women globally.

Looking to Join Us in our Next Anthology or Publish YOUR Own?

She Rises Studios Publishing offers full-service publishing, marketing, book tour, and campaign services. For more information, contact info@sherisesstudios.com

We are always looking for women who want to share their stories and expertise and feature their businesses on our podcasts, in our books, and in our magazines.

SEE WHAT WE DO

OUR PODCAST	OUR BOOKS	OUR SERVICES

Be featured in the Becoming An Unstoppable Woman magazine, published in 13 countries and sold in all major retailers. Get the visibility you need to LEVEL UP in your business!

Have your own TV show streamed across major platforms like Roku TV, Amazon Fire Stick, Apple TV and more!

Learn to leverage your expertise. Build your online presence and grow your audience with FENIX TV.

https://fenixtv.sherisesstudios.com/

Visit www.SheRisesStudios.com to see how YOU can join the #BAUW movement and help your community to achieve the UNSTOPPABLE mindset.

Have you checked out the *She Rises Studios Podcast?*

Find us on all MAJOR platforms: Spotify, IHeartRadio, Apple Podcasts, Google Podcasts, etc.

Looking to become a sponsor or build a partnership?

Email us at info@sherisesstudios.com

SHE RISES
STUDIOS

www.ingramcontent.com/pod-product-compliance
Lightning Source LLC
Chambersburg PA
CBHW070919120626
46546CB00001B/323